A Guide to
The Finance (No 2) Act 1997

Previous titles in the series

A Guide to the Leasehold Reform, Housing and Urban
    Development Act 1993
A Guide to the Criminal Justice and Public Order Act 1994
A Guide to the Finance Act 1994
A Guide to the Police and Magistrates' Courts Act 1994
A Guide to the Sunday Trading Act 1994
A Guide to the Trade Marks Act 1994
A Guide to the Finance Act 1995
A Guide to the Pensions Act 1995
A Guide to the Criminal Procedure and Investigations Act 1996
A Guide to the Family Law Act 1996
A Guide to the Finance Act 1996
A Guide to the Housing Act 1996
A Guide to the Finance Act 1997
A Guide to the Crime (Sentences) Act 1997

A GUIDE TO
THE FINANCE (No 2) ACT
1997

(excluding provisions relating to excise duties and
certain miscellaneous provisions not relating to taxation)

Contributors
COLIN DAVIS, MA, FCA
ZIGURDS KRONBERGS, MA, BSc, ARCS, ACA, FCCA
ROBERT MURGATROYD, formerly one of HM Inspectors of Taxes
GEOFF PENNELLS, FCCA, ATII
IAN PURVES, FCA, ATII, APMI
GARY RICHARDS, MA, LLB, ATII, Solicitor
CHARLES VITEZ, FCA
RICHARD WALLINGTON, MA, Barrister

BUTTERWORTHS
LONDON, EDINBURGH, DUBLIN
1997

United Kingdom	Butterworths, a Division of Reed Elsevier (UK) Ltd, Halsbury House, 35 Chancery Lane, LONDON WC2A 1EL and 4 Hill Street, EDINBURGH EH2 3JZ
Australia	Butterworths Pty Ltd, SYDNEY, MELBOURNE, BRISBANE, ADELAIDE, PERTH, CANBERRA and HOBART
Canada	Butterworth Canada Ltd, TORONTO and VANCOUVER
Ireland	Butterworth (Ireland) Ltd, DUBLIN
Malaysia	Malayan Law Journal Sdn Bhd, KUALA LUMPUR
New Zealand	Butterworths of New Zealand Ltd, WELLINGTON and AUCKLAND
Singapore	Reed Elsevier (Singapore) Pte Ltd, SINGAPORE
South Africa	Butterworth Publishers (Pty) Ltd, DURBAN
USA	Michie Butterworth, CHARLOTTESVILLE, Virginia

©

Reed Elsevier (UK) Ltd
1997

A CIP Catalogue record for this book is available from the British Library.

ISBN 0 406 89885 5

Typeset, printed and bound in Great Britain by William Clowes Ltd, Beccles and London.

RELEVANT DATES

2 July 1997   Budget Statement
7 July 1997   Publication of Finance Bill
31 July 1997   Royal Assent

CONTENTS

INTRODUCTION

THE WINDFALL TAX

This is a one-off tax charged on certain privatised utility companies. The measure of the windfall in any case is the difference between the earn-out value of the company (the "value in profit-making terms") and the value based on the price at which the shares were offered on flotation. The earn-out value is nine times the average annual profits of the earn-out period (usually the period of four financial years of the company immediately following flotation). The tax is charged at the rate of 23 per cent and is payable in two equal instalments on 1 December 1997 and 1 December 1998 respectively (ss 1, 2 and Sch 1).

The tax is under the care and management of the Board of Inland Revenue. The relevant provisions of TMA 1970 (returns, assessments, appeals, payment of tax, interest, penalties and information powers) are applied for windfall tax purposes (s 3 and Sch 2).

Windfall tax may be deducted in computing the distributable profit pool for the purposes of profit-related pay (s 4). Various terms are defined for windfall tax purposes (s 5).

VALUE ADDED TAX AND EXCISE DUTIES

Value added tax.   The rate of VAT chargeable on fuel and power for domestic use is reduced to five per cent as from 1 September 1997 (s 6).

Alcoholic liquor duties.   The duty on spirits is increased to £19.56 per hectolitre of alcohol in the spirits as from 1 January 1998 (s 7). The duty on beer is increased to £11.14 per hectolitre as from 1 January 1998 (s 8). The duties on wine are also increased as from 1 January 1998 (s 9 substituting a new table of rates in Sch 1 of the Alcoholic Liquor Duties Act 1979). Finally, the rates of duty on cider are increased as from 1 January 1998 (s 10).

Hydrocarbon oil duties.   The rates of duty on light oil and heavy oil are increased to 45.1p per litre and 40.28p per litre respectively as from 2 July 1997. The rates of rebate on heavy oil, gas oil and light oil for furnace fuel are increased to 2p per litre, 2.58p per litre and 2p per litre respectively (s 11).

Tobacco products duty.   The rates of duty are increased as from 1 December 1997 (s 12 introducing a new table in Sch 1 of the Tobacco Products Duty Act 1979).

Vehicle excise and registration.   The rate of duty on private cars and other vehicles in the same category is increased to £150 as from 15 November 1997. The rates of duty on rigid goods vehicles and tractive units are also increased as from 15 November 1997 (s 13 and new tables in the Vehicle Excise and Registration Act 1994 Sch 1 paras 9, 11).

Customs and Excise may charge fleet operators and motor manufacturers for the cost of setting up electronic links with the DVLA and the cost of processing licensing applications electronically (s 14).

INCOME TAX AND CORPORATION TAX

Reliefs for interest and private medical insurance. The rate of tax relief on mortgage interest is reduced to ten per cent as from 1998–99 (s 15). The upper limit for qualifying loans remains £30,000 for 1998–99 (s 16).

Relief under FA 1989 s 54 for medical insurance premiums is not available for premiums paid—

(*a*) under a contract entered into on or after 2 July 1997; or

(*b*) generally on or after 6 April 1999.

There is transitional relief under (*a*) for certain contracts written up to 31 July 1997 where the proposal was received by the insurer before 2 July 1997 or where the contract is a renewal of a contract which expired before 2 July 1997 (s 17).

Corporation tax. The main rate of corporation tax for the financial year 1997 (year to 31 March 1998) is reduced to 31 per cent and the small companies rate is reduced to 21 per cent. Existing assessments will be adjusted accordingly (s 18).

Dividends, tax credits etc on and after 2nd July 1997. "Pension funds" are no longer entitled to the payment of tax credits on UK company dividends and other qualifying distributions. This applies in respect of distributions made on or after 2 July 1997. Pension funds include investments held by life assurance companies etc in respect of their retirement annuity contracts and personal pension schemes. Where income of a pension fund is brought into charge to tax (eg because the scheme is over-funded), the tax credits to be set off against the tax liability are limited to tax credits on income brought within the charge to tax. Thus tax credits on dividends covered by the exemption are not available against the tax payable on unfranked income which is chargeable to tax (TA 1988 s 19 and new s 231A).

For accounting periods beginning on or after 2 July 1997, it is not possible to set off trading losses against surplus franked investment income under TA 1988 s 242 or s 243. Further, where there has been such a set off in the past, and there is a surplus of franked payments in an accounting period beginning on or after 2 July 1997, there is no longer any adjustment to restore the loss and adjust the set off of ACT. For an accounting period which straddles 2 July 1997, the surplus FII available for set off is restricted to the amount arising up to 1 July 1997 (s 20).

Where the personal representatives of a deceased estate receive a non-qualifying distribution which is used to fund payments to beneficiaries, the beneficiaries are now treated, in relation to such payments, as having received income with a non repayable tax credit covering income tax at the lower rate. This applies in relation to amounts which the beneficiary is deemed to receive, or has a right to receive, on or after 2 July 1997 (s 21).

An individual Lloyd's Name is no longer entitled to a tax credit on UK company distributions from shares held as part of his premiums trust fund.

Distributions received by corporate members of Lloyd's from assets forming part of their ancillary trust funds or other underwriting business funds are now taxed as trading receipts. There is no longer a repayable tax credit on such distributions. This applies to distributions made on or after 2 July 1997 (s 22).

Insurance companies are not entitled to the payment of tax credits on UK company distributions made after 2 July 1997 which relate to pensions business. All UK company distributions are to be included in the computation of the profits or a company's life assurance business under Schedule D Case I. There are numerous consequential amendments to the legislation relating to insurance companies (TA 1988 s 23 and Sch 3, amending ss 431–458A and Sch 19AC).

The provisions of TA 1988 s 95 (which relate to special dividends and the distributions which arise when a company purchases its own shares) are extended to cover all distributions from UK companies. Such distributions are, therefore, treated as trading receipts in the hands of a dealer in securities as from 2 July 1997. The same applies to payments "representative of" such distributions (ie manufactured dividends). In particular, dividends on fixed rate preference shares are now caught by this provision. Manufactured dividends paid by dealers are now Case I expenses (s 24).

A new definition of "fixed rate preference shares" is inserted into TA 1988 Sch 28B. Various references to the old definition are changed so as to refer to the new one. The new definition is the same as the old one (s 25).

In consequence of the above changes, the dividend stripping provisions of TA 1988 s 732 are no longer to apply to the purchase and resale of securities if the dividend received by the purchaser is treated as a Case I receipt. The existing exclusion for market makers etc is no longer relevant and is repealed. The existing exclusion relating to overseas securities is widened to include securities issued by any body of persons not resident in the UK. The changes apply where the distribution is received by the purchaser on or after 2 July 1997 (s 26).

A new s 687A is inserted into TA 1988 to stop companies from effectively getting payment of tax credits by routing UK company dividends through discretionary trusts. Under s 687, income payments by trustees to beneficiaries are treated as annual payments. Accordingly, s 687A(3) provides that such payments are excluded from the charge to corporation tax, but that any tax deducted or deemed to be deducted is not available for set off against the company's corporation tax liability or the tax for which it must account on its annual payments. This applies to payments made on or after 2 July 1997 (s 27).

A new s 231B is inserted into TA 1988 to forestall attempts to get around the above rules by setting up arrangements whereby distributions are routed indirectly to a pension fund or company which would not be entitled to a tax credit if it received the distribution directly. Bona fide commercial transactions are not caught. The immediate recipient of the distribution from the company is prevented from claiming payment of any tax credit on the distribution or regarding that distribution as franked investment income. The Revenue accept that ordinary stock lending arrangements and repos are bona fide commercial arrangements as is the use of derivatives at open market rates as part of the efficient management of a portfolio of investments (s 28).

UK company distributions received by unauthorised unit trusts between 2 July 1997 and 6 April 1999 are treated as Foreign Income Dividends in the hands of the recipient. This means that if the distributions are paid to unit holders, the trustees must deduct income tax at the basic rate from the payment, there being no grossing up for tax credits. This does not apply if the unit trust is a court common investment fund or is a charitable body within TA 1988 s 505 , a heritage body under s 507 or a scientific research organisation under s 508. The purpose of this provision is to forestall attempts by pension funds to hold their equity investments through the medium of unauthorised unit trusts (s 29). After 5 April 1999, the new rules set out below apply.

The rate of tax credit on UK company distributions is reduced from 1/4 to 1/9 of the distribution as from 6 April 1999. There is, however, no corresponding reduction in the rate of ACT. From the same date, UK companies will cease to be entitled to a payment of tax credit under TA 1988 s 231(2) by reason of any exemption. Persons other than UK resident companies are entitled to set tax credits against their UK tax liability, but only to the extent that the distributions are brought into charge to UK tax. Thus pension funds will cease to be entitled to the payment of tax credits generally. Thereupon, the provisions of s 231A which are introduced by s 19 above cease to have effect. The new rules will not prevent the payment of tax credits to non-residents under the provisions of a double taxation agreement (s 30).

Where Schedule F income is chargeable to income tax at the lower rate rather than at the basic rate, in accordance with TA 1988 s 1A, it will be charged at the rate of ten per cent (the Schedule F ordinary rate) as from 6 April 1999. This tax liability will be discharged by the ten per cent tax credit mentioned above. Where the income is otherwise chargeable at the higher rate, it will be charged at the rate of 32.5 per cent (the Schedule F upper rate). Thus a dividend of £80 grosses up to £88.89 and the tax liability is 32.5 per cent of £88.89 = £28.89, less tax credit of £8.89 = £20, leaving a net of tax dividend of £60, which is the same as under the present regime. The same rule applies to equivalent foreign income chargeable under Schedule D Case V (s 31).

As far as discretionary trusts are concerned, Schedule F income which would otherwise be taxed at the rate applicable to trusts (currently 34 per cent) is to be taxed at 25 per cent (the Schedule F trust rate) as from 6 April 1999. Thus a dividend of £80 grosses up to £88.89 and the tax liability is 25 per cent of £88.89 = £22.22, less tax credit £8.89 = £13.33. This leaves a net of tax dividend of £66.67, compared with £66 at present. The same applies to other "Schedule F type income" such as equivalent foreign income, non-qualifying distributions etc. Where a qualifying distribution arises to trustees on the redemption, repayment or purchase by a company of its own shares, that distribution is treated as Schedule F income within TA 1988 s 686 .This rule does not apply to income already caught under subs (2)(a) or to income treated as that of the settlor. Charitable trusts and pension fund trusts are also excluded as they are dealt with under other sections (s 32).

As regards the estate of a deceased person in the course of administration, payments to beneficiaries out of Schedule F income are deemed to have borne tax at the Schedule F ordinary rate rather than at the lower rate (new s 698A)

4

and are deemed to be Schedule F income of the beneficiaries. This applies as from 6 April 1999. Such income is deemed to be brought into charge to tax for the purposes of TA 1988 ss 348, 349 . There are consequential amendments to s 701 (interpretation) (s 33).

There are numerous detailed consequential amendments to the legislation. In particular, the rules for calculating a company's liability to ACT when it receives franked investment income are changed to ensure that the ACT liability is not increased as a result of the reduction of the rate of tax credit on UK company dividends (Sch 4 paras 8, 9). "Franked payment" means the distribution plus the tax credit attaching thereto. The ACT is calculated at 9/10ths of the ACT rate on the excess of franked payments over FII. For example, an excess of £100 represents a distribution of £90 plus a tax credit of ten pounds. The ACT is 9/10 x 1/4 x £100, which is the same as 1/4 x £90. Where a close company loan to a participator is released, the amount released is treated as income received net of ten per cent tax rather than net of 20 per cent tax (s 34 and Sch 4).

Charities are granted transitional relief in respect of UK company distributions received between 6 April 1999 and 5 April 2004, provided the distributions are applied for charitable purposes. They may claim payment from the Board the following percentages of the distributions—

year	%
1999-00	21
2000-01	17
2001-02	13
2002-03	8
2003-04	4

The same applies to heritage bodies falling within TA 1988 s 507 and scientific research associations falling within s 508. Claims must be made within two years after the end of the chargeable period. There is a right of appeal to the Special Commissioners against a refusal of a claim. If the charity etc owns ten per cent or more of any class of shares in a company, distributions on those shares which are payable out of pre-acquisition profits do not qualify for the above payments. Payments in respect of bonus issues which are treated as a distribution are restricted to that part of the distribution which represents a normal commercial return on the consideration given for the shares (s 35 and Sch 5).

The Foreign Income Dividend scheme is being brought to an end on 5 April 1999. No distributions made after that date are to be treated as FIDs. However, the 1998 Finance Bill will include special provisions for international headquarters companies. The existing adaptation of the FID scheme to company purchases of own shares will no longer be required in view of the general abolition of tax credits for pension funds etc. References to FIDs in other parts of the legislation are repealed as from 6 April 1999 (s 36 and Sch 6).

Gilt-edged securities. As from 6 April 1998, interest on registered gilts (as defined in TCGA 1992 Sch 9) is to be paid gross. The holder may request that income tax be deducted at source under TA 1988 s 50(2). Any previous application under that section will continue in force unless withdrawn by the holder. In consequence of the above, s 51A is no longer required and is repealed as from 6 April 1998. There are consequential amendments to the legislation relating to periodic accounting for tax deducted at source on payment of interest on gilts (ss 37, 38).

Relief for losses etc. Under TA 1988 s 393A , trading losses may be carried back for a period of three years for corporation tax purposes. That period is reduced to a period of twelve months in relation to any loss sustained in an accounting period ending on or after 2 July 1997. However, the period of three years is retained for terminal losses and for losses resulting from the special allowances given for the costs of decommissioning North sea oil and gas installations. In relation to a loss arising in an accounting period straddling 2 July 1997, that part of the loss which is apportioned to the period up to 1 July 1997 may be carried back three years. The apportionment is on a time basis unless that would be unjust or unreasonable in any particular case, in which case the apportionment is on a just and reasonable basis. Excess trading charges may be deducted in computing a terminal loss. The transfer of a trade which falls within TA 1988 s 343 (transfer without change of control) does not entitle the transferor to claim terminal loss relief in respect of the trade transferred (s 39).

Under FA 1996 s 83(2)(*c*) and Sch 8 para 3, non-trade deficits on loan relationships may be carried back for a period of three years for set off against Case III profits on loan relationships. This three year period is reduced to a period of twelve months for deficits arising in accounting periods ending on or after 2 July 1997. Where a deficit arises in a period straddling that date, it is apportioned on a time basis to the period up to 1 July 1997 and the period from 2 July 1997. The first part may be carried back to 1 April 1996 (on which date the loan relationship provisions came into effect). There are corresponding provisions relating to insurance companies (s 40).

The group relief provisions are tightened up in cases where—

(*a*) a company claims relief in a particular accounting period for losses etc surrendered by more than one company; or

(*b*) a company surrenders losses etc for a particular accounting period to more than one claimant company,

and the accounting periods of the claimant and surrendering companies overlap but are not identical.

In (*a*), the total relief which may be claimed for the period of overlap is limited to the proportion of its profits which are attributable to that period of overlap. In (*b*), the total amount of losses etc which may be surrendered in respect of the period of overlap is limited to the proportion of the surrendering company's losses etc which are attributable to that period of overlap. Apportionments are to be made on a time basis unless in a particular case that would be unjust or unreasonable, in which case a just and reasonable basis is adopted (s 41 and Sch 7 inserting new s 403A into TA 1988).

The restrictions apply to accounting periods of claimant or surrendering companies which end on or after 2 July 1997, but not in respect of periods of overlap which end before that date (Sch 7 para 9). Where a period of overlap straddles 2 July 1997, profits and losses are apportioned on a time basis to the period up to 1 July 1997 and the period from 2 July 1997. The old rules apply to the former period (Sch 7 para 9).

Capital allowances for small and medium sized businesses.   Capital expenditure on machinery and plant, where incurred by a small company or small business between 2 July 1997 and 1 July 1998, qualifies for a first year allowance of 50 per cent except in relation to long life assets where the rate is 12 per cent. These new rates do not apply to expenditure on cars, ships, railway assets, machinery and plant for leasing or assets excluded from the rules on long life assets under the transitional provisions. There is also a "main benefit" exclusion where the provision of the asset is connected with a change in the nature or conduct of a trade or business carried on by a person other than the person incurring the expenditure (s 42).

A company is "small" if it qualifies as a small or medium sized company under the Companies Act 1985 s 247. This means that it must satisfy two of the following conditions—

(*a*) its turnover for its financial year in which the expenditure is incurred is not more than £11.2 million;

(*b*) its assets do not exceed £5.6 million;

(*c*) it has not more than 250 employees.

Where the company is a member of a group, the group must be "small". An unincorporated business is "small" if, had it been carried on by a company, that company would be "small" within the above definition. There are anti-avoidance provisions to counteract arrangements whereby a small company may become a member of a large group (CAA 1990 s 43 and new s 22A).

Capital allowances and finance leases.   Finance lessors of machinery and plant may claim only a proportion of the normal writing down allowances for the accounting period in which expenditure is incurred. This is achieved by bringing only a proportion of the expenditure into its capital allowances computation for that period and the balance in the next period. The proportion is the fraction of the accounting period from the date the expenditure was incurred to the end of the period. Thus if a lessor with a 31 December year end incurs expenditure on 10 December 1997, then only 22/365ths of the expenditure will qualify for allowances in 1997 (s 44). Where the finance lessor acquires the assets under a "hire purchase agreement" falling within CAA 1990 s 60, he is treated as incurring the expenditure when it is actually incurred and not, as at present, all at the commencement of the agreement (s 45). These rules apply to expenditure incurred on or after 2 July 1997, unless incurred under a contract entered into before that date in which case they apply to expenditure incurred up to 1 July 1998.

There is a further restriction on capital allowances available to a finance lessor of machinery and plant where the lease arises as part of a sale and lease-back arrangement. The lessor's qualifying expenditure is restricted to the seller's written down value (rather than to the seller's cost as at present under CAA 1990 s 75). In calculating the seller's written down value, it is assumed that the seller claimed any allowances which he was entitled to claim. No allowances are available to the lessor if the leasing arrangements are such that he does not bear any risk of non-payment of rents etc. The expenditure on which a future purchaser of the lessor's interest may claim is restricted to the disposal value of the person from whom he purchases that interest, which cannot exceed the amount on which that person claims capital allowances.

7

Finally, the existing restrictions of s 75(1)-(3) are widened to include the case where machinery and plant is leased under a finance lease to a person carrying on non-trading activities, such as a public authority (CAA 1990 s 46 and new s 76A). "Finance lease" is defined in a new CAA 1990 s 82A. Broadly, it is any lease treated as a finance lease under SSAP 21 (s 47).

Films.   Expenditure incurred between 2 July 1997 and 1 July 2000 on the production or acquisition of a film may be written off in full in the accounting period in which the film is completed or acquired, provided that the total production expenditure on the film does not exceed £15 million and the film is completed on or after 2 July 1997. However, in the case of an acquisition, if the acquisition cost exceeds the production cost, then the 100 per cent write off applies only to an amount equal to the production cost. The balance is written off in accordance with F(No2)A 1992 s 42. The Revenue may impose an arm's length price in the case of transactions between connected persons (s 48).

MISCELLANEOUS AND SUPPLEMENTARY

Stamp duty.   The rates of ad valorem duty payable under the heading "conveyance or transfer on sale of any property", which are set out in FA 1963 s 55 , are amended as follows—

consideration	rate
up to £60,000	nil
£60,001 to £250,000	1%
£250,001 to £500,000	1.5%
over £500,000	2%

The new rates apply to instruments executed on or after 8 July 1997, except for instruments executed in persuance of contracts made on or before 2 July 1997. The appropriate certification under FA 1958 s 34(4) is required where the nil, 1 per cent or 1.5 per cent rates are to apply. The rate of duty on transfers of stocks and shares remains 0.5 per cent (s 49).

Provisional collection of taxes.   The provisions of the Provisional Collection of Taxes Act 1968 are amended so that Budget resolutions passed in February or March remain effective until 5 August. It will be appreciated that future Budgets are to be delivered in the spring (s 50).

Supplemental.   These provisions follow the usual pattern (ss 51-53).

FINANCE (NO 2) ACT 1997
(1997 Chapter 58)

ARRANGEMENT OF SECTIONS

PART I
THE WINDFALL TAX

PART II
VALUE ADDED TAX AND EXCISE DUTIES

Value added tax

PART III
INCOME TAX AND CORPORATION TAX

Reliefs for interest and private medical insurance

Corporation tax

Distributions, tax credits etc on and after 2nd July 1997

Distributions, tax credits etc: avoidance

Distributions, tax credits etc in and after 1999–00

PART IV
MISCELLANEOUS AND SUPPLEMENTAL

An Act to grant certain duties, to alter other duties, and to amend the law relating to the National Debt and the Public Revenue, and to make further provision in connection with Finance. [31st July 1997]

PART I
THE WINDFALL TAX

1 Charge to windfall tax

(1) Every company which, on 2nd July 1997, was benefitting from a windfall from the flotation of an undertaking whose privatisation involved the imposition of economic regulation shall be charged with a tax (to be known as the "windfall tax") on the amount of that windfall.

(2) Windfall tax shall be charged at the rate of 23 per cent.

(3) Schedule 1 to this Act (which sets out how to quantify the windfall from which a company was benefitting on 2nd July 1997) shall have effect.

GENERAL NOTE

The windfall tax is a one-off tax, payable in two instalments, charged on certain privatised utility companies. Essentially, each such company has to calculate an "earn-out" value of its shares (known as a value "in profit-making terms") and pay tax at 23 per cent on the difference between that earn-out value and the value based on the flotation price of its shares on privatisation (known as the "value for privatisation purposes"). This difference, which would be the earn-out consideration in a private sale, is the "windfall" which gives the tax its name. However, the tax is payable by the companies rather than by the purchasers of the shares.

Schedule 1 sets out the basis of computation of the tax liability.

2 The companies benefitting from windfalls

(1) For the purposes of this Part a company in existence on 2nd July 1997 was benefitting on that date from a windfall from the flotation of an undertaking whose privatisation involved the imposition of economic regulation if—

(*a*) that company, or a company of which it was on that date a demerged successor, had before that date been privatised by means of a flotation;

(*b*) there had, before that flotation, been a statutory transfer of property, rights and liabilities from a public corporation to the floated company or to a company which, at the time of the flotation, was a subsidiary undertaking of the floated company; and

(*c*) at the time of the flotation, the floated company was carrying on an undertaking whose privatisation involved the imposition of economic regulation.

(2) For the purposes of this Part a company was privatised by means of a flotation if—

(*a*) an offer of shares in that company was at any time made to the public in the United Kingdom;

(*b*) the shares which were the subject-matter of the offer were publicly-owned at the time of the offer;

(*c*) the offer was or included an offer of shares for disposal at a fixed price; and

(*d*) shares in that company were first admitted to listing on the Official List of the Stock Exchange in pursuance of an application made in connection with the offer.

(3) In this Part references, in relation to a company privatised by means of a flotation, to the time of the company's flotation are references to the time when shares in the floated company were first admitted to listing on the Official List of the Stock Exchange.

(4) For the purposes of this Part a company in existence on 2nd July 1997 ("the relevant company") was on that date a demerged successor of a company privatised by means of a flotation if—

(a) after the flotation of the floated company but before 2nd July 1997, there had been a statutory transfer of property, rights and liabilities from the floated company to a company ("the transferee company") which was a subsidiary undertaking of the floated company at the time of the transfer;

(b) the transferee company was not a subsidiary undertaking of the floated company on 2nd July 1997 but was, on that date, a subsidiary undertaking of the relevant company; and

(c) before 2nd July 1997 shares in the relevant company had been admitted to listing on the Official List of the Stock Exchange in pursuance of an application made in connection with the transaction, or series of transactions, by virtue of which the transferee company ceased to be a subsidiary undertaking of the floated company.

(5) For the purposes of this section a company was, at the time of its flotation, carrying on an undertaking whose privatisation involved the imposition of economic regulation, if that company, or a company which at that time was a subsidiary undertaking of that company, was at that time—

(a) a public telecommunications operator, within the meaning of the Telecommunications Act 1984;

(b) an airport operator in relation to an airport subject to economic regulation under Part IV of the Airports Act 1986;

(c) the holder of an authorisation granted under section 7 of the Gas Act 1986, as originally enacted (public gas suppliers);

(d) the holder of an appointment under section 11 of the Water Act 1989 as the water undertaker for any area of England and Wales;

(e) the holder of a licence granted under section 6 of the Electricity Act 1989 or Article 10 of the Electricity (Northern Ireland) Order 1992 (licences authorising generation, transmission and supply of electricity); or

(f) a company authorised by a licence under section 8 of the Railways Act 1993 to be the operator of a railway asset.

(6) In subsection (5) above "airport operator" has the same meaning as in the Airports Act 1986.

GENERAL NOTE

This section sets out the rules for identifying the companies liable to the tax. They are companies subject to economic regulation following the privatisation of the undertakings which they carry on.

First, it is necessary to identify the privatised undertakings acquired by companies which then floated on the Stock Exchange. They are identified in sub-s (5) by reference to certain Acts of Parliament. They comprise telecommunications companies, airport operators, gas supply companies, water companies, electricity companies and railway operators.

Next, it is necessary to identify the companies carrying on those undertakings on 2 July 1997. They are the chargeable companies. They might be the original companies which were floated or successors of such companies.

3   Administration of the windfall tax etc

(1) The windfall tax shall be under the care and management of the Commissioners of Inland Revenue.

(2) Schedule 2 to this Act (which makes provision with respect to the management and collection of the windfall tax) shall have effect.

(3) Subject to paragraph 19(5) of Schedule 8 to the Taxes Act 1988 (which is the provision about profit-related pay schemes that is amended by section 4 below), nothing in this Act or the Tax Acts shall have the effect of allowing or requiring any amount of windfall tax to be deducted in computing income, profits or losses for any of the purposes of the Tax Acts.

GENERAL NOTE

The administration of the windfall tax is under the care and management of the Board of Inland Revenue. Schedule 2 gives details of the administration of the tax.

Windfall tax is not deductible in computing income, profits or losses for corporation tax purposes.

4   The windfall tax and profit-related pay

(1) In paragraph 19 of Schedule 8 to the Taxes Act 1988 (ascertainment of profits for the purposes of profit-related pay schemes)—

(*a*) in sub-paragraph (5)(*b*), after "1985" there shall be inserted "or section 3(3) of the Finance (No 2) Act 1997"; and

(*b*) after paragraph (*ff*) of sub-paragraph (6) there shall be inserted the following paragraph—

"(*fg*) windfall tax charged under Part I of the Finance (No 2) Act 1997;".

(2) Subsection (1) above has effect in relation to the preparation, for the purposes of any scheme, of a profit and loss account for any period ending on or after 2nd July 1997.

(3) Subsection (1) above shall not have effect in relation to an existing scheme unless, before the end of the period of six months beginning with the day on which this Act is passed, the scheme is altered, with effect for all periods ending on or after 2nd July 1997, to take account of that subsection.

(4) Provision made, in compliance with paragraph 20(1) of Schedule 8 to the Taxes Act 1988 (consistency in preparation of accounts), by any existing scheme that is altered to take account of subsection (1) above shall not prevent a profit and loss account from being prepared in accordance with the alteration.

(5) An alteration of an existing scheme to take account of subsection (1) above shall be treated as being within section 177B of the Taxes Act 1988 (alterations which are registrable and which, when registered, cannot give rise to the Board's power of cancellation).

(6) In this section "existing scheme" means a scheme which at any time in the period beginning with 2nd July 1997 and ending immediately before the day

on which this Act is passed was a registered scheme under Chapter III of Part V of the Taxes Act 1988.

(7) The preceding provisions of this section shall cease to have effect, in accordance with the notes to Part VI(3) of Schedule 18 to the Finance Act 1997, as if they were included in the repeal of Schedule 8 to the Taxes Act 1988.

GENERAL NOTE

Windfall tax may be deducted in computing the distributable pool for any period ending on or after 2 July 1997 if the company so wishes and the scheme rules are amended as necessary.

5 Interpretation of Part I

(1) In this Part—

"company" means a company within the meaning of the Companies Act 1985 or the Companies (Northern Ireland) Order 1986;

"fixed price", in relation to any offer of publicly-owned shares in a company, means—

(*a*) a price set out in the offer, or

(*b*) a price subsequently fixed by a Minister of the Crown in a case in which the amount of a first instalment of the price was fixed by the offer;

"the floated company", in relation to the privatisation of a company by means of a flotation, means the company so privatised;

"public corporation", in relation to a statutory transfer, means any body corporate in existence at the time of the transfer which—

(*a*) had been established by or in accordance with the provisions of any enactment; and

(*b*) had a membership consisting of, or including, persons appointed as members by a Minister of the Crown;

"publicly-owned", in relation to any shares, means held by—

(*a*) a Minister of the Crown or the Treasury; or

(*b*) a nominee for a Minister of the Crown or for the Treasury;

"share" includes any right to require the issue of a share;

"statutory transfer" means a transfer under a transferring enactment or by or in accordance with a statutory scheme;

"subsidiary undertaking"—

(*a*) except in relation to a company formed and registered in Northern Ireland, means a subsidiary undertaking within the meaning of Part VII of the Companies Act 1985; and

(*b*) in relation to a company so formed and registered, means a subsidiary undertaking within the meaning of Part VIII of the Companies (Northern Ireland) Order 1986.

(2) In this section—

"enactment" means an enactment contained in a public general Act or any provision of Northern Ireland legislation;

"Minister of the Crown" includes a Northern Ireland department or the head of such a department;

"statutory scheme" means any scheme which—

(*a*) has been made in exercise of any power or duty conferred or imposed by any enactment;

(*b*) contains provision for the division of property, rights and liabilities between different persons, or for the transfer of property, rights and liabilities to a company; and

(*c*) would not have taken effect or come into force but for having been approved by a Minister of the Crown;

"transferring enactment" means an enactment under which property, rights and liabilities of a person specified in the enactment became, by virtue of that enactment, the property, rights or liabilities of a company nominated under that enactment.

(3) In subsection (2) above the reference, in relation to a scheme, to its having been approved by a Minister of the Crown includes a reference to its having been made by a Minister of the Crown.

(4) The reference in subsection (1) above to Part VII of the Companies Act 1985 shall be construed, in relation to times in relation to which that Part had effect without the amendments made by the Companies Act 1989, as if those amendments did have effect in relation to those times.

GENERAL NOTE

This section sets out the definitions of various terms.

PART II

VALUE ADDED TAX AND EXCISE DUTIES

Value added tax

6 Fuel and power for domestic or charity use

(1) In section 2(1A) of the Value Added Tax Act 1994 (rate of VAT on fuel and power for domestic use etc), for "8 per cent" there shall be substituted "5 per cent.".

(2) This section applies in relation to any supply made on or after 1st September 1997 and any acquisition or importation taking place on or after that date.

GENERAL NOTE

The rate of VAT on fuel and power for domestic use and charity non-business use has been reduced from 8% to 5%, the lowest rate possible under EC law. The change will take effect from 1 September 1997. The special rules for domestic fuel and power are set out in VATA 1994 Schedule A1 and the rate is set in VATA 1994 s 2(1A).

PART III

Reliefs for interest and private medical insurance

15 Mortgage interest payments

(1) In section 353 of the Taxes Act 1988 (general provision for relief for interest payments), in subsection (1G) (amount of relief for interest on loans to buy land, etc), for paragraph (*a*) there shall be substituted—

"(*a*) in relation to so much of any interest as is eligible for relief under this section by virtue of section 354, means 10 per cent; and".

(2) In section 369 of that Act (deduction at source of mortgage interest relief), in subsection (1A) (percentage of interest deductible), for paragraph (*a*) there shall be substituted—

"(*a*) in relation to so much of any payment of relevant loan interest as is not a payment in relation to which paragraph (*b*) below has effect, means 10 per cent; and".

(3) Subsection (1) above has effect in relation to any payment of interest (whenever falling due) made in the year 1998-99 or any subsequent year of assessment; and subsection (2) above has effect in relation to any payment of interest which becomes due in the year 1998-99 or any subsequent year of assessment.

BACKGROUND NOTE

Before 6 April 1991, relief for qualifying mortgage interest payments was by deduction in computing the taxpayer's total income, so that relief was given at the marginal rate of tax. For years from 1991–92 onwards, FA 1991 s 27 restricted the relief to the basic rate of income tax (then 25 per cent). The rate at which relief was given was further reduced in two stages by FA 1994 s 81: for interest paid in 1994–95, relief was to be at the rate of 20 per cent and, from 6 April 1995, at 15 per cent.

GENERAL NOTE

This section continues the trend to further reduction and, in all likelihood, eventual abolition, of mortgage interest relief, by reducing the rate at which relief is given to 10 per cent, with effect from 6 April 1998 (sub-s (1)).

Where relief is given under s 353 (ie not under MIRAS), it is by a reduction of income tax, which is the smaller of—

(*a*) 10 per cent of the interest eligible for relief; and
(*b*) the taxpayer's liability to income tax
(s 353(1G), as amended by sub-s (1)).

This applies to all payments of interest made after 5 April 1998, whenever falling due (sub-s (3)).

Where relief is given by deduction at source under MIRAS it will, from 6 April 1998, be by deduction of 10 per cent from the relevant loan interest (TA 1988 s 369(1A), as amended by sub-s (2)). In this case, the amendment applies to all interest becoming due after 5 April 1998 (sub-s (3)).

QUALIFYING MAXIMUM

There is no change to the "qualifying maximum", which remains £30,000 (see s 16 below).

MORTGAGE-LINKED LIFE ANNUITIES

There is no change to the rate of relief on interest payments enjoyed by borrowers of age 65 and over who have borrowed against the security of their home to purchase life annuities. They continue to receive relief at the basic rate of income tax (ss 353(1G)(*b*), 365), as they have done since 6 April 1991 although, of course, the basic rate has itself fallen from 25 per cent at that time to 23 per cent currently.

16   Limit on relief for interest for 1998-99

For the year 1998-99 the qualifying maximum defined in section 367(5) of the Taxes Act 1988 (limit on relief for interest on certain loans) shall be £30,000.

GENERAL NOTE

The "qualifying maximum" (the maximum amount on which mortgage interest payable is eligible for relief) needs to be set each year. This section sets the qualifying maximum in advance for 1998–99 at £30,000, at which level it has remained since 6 April 1983. It has already been set at £30,000 for the current year, 1997–98, by FA 1997 s 57.

The qualifying maximum applies, broadly, to loans for the purchase of an only or main residence or taken out by those aged 65 and over to purchase a life annuity.

At an average mortgage rate of 7.75 per cent, the maximum amount of interest qualifying for relief is accordingly £2,325. With relief restricted to 10 per cent from 6 April 1998, the actual maximum relief at this rate of interest would be £232.50 per annum.

17   Withdrawal of relief on medical insurance premiums

(1) Subject to subsections (2) and (3) below, relief under section 54 of the Finance Act 1989 (medical insurance) shall not be given in respect of any payment where either—

(*a*) the premium in respect of which the payment is made is a premium under a contract entered into on or after 2nd July 1997; or

(*b*) the payment is received by the insurer on or after 6th April 1999.

(2) Subsection (1) above shall not affect the giving of relief in respect of a payment received by an insurer before 6th April 1999 where—

(*a*) the premium in respect of which the payment is made is a premium under a contract entered into on or after 2nd July 1997 but before 1st August 1997;

(*b*) the contract is one entered into in pursuance of a written proposal received by or on behalf of the insurer before 2nd July 1997;

(*c*) the contract is not a contract entered into by way of the renewal of an earlier contract; and

(*d*) if the payment is not itself a payment received before 1st August 1997, the insurer had before 1st August 1997 received an earlier payment in respect of a premium under the contract in question.

(3) Subsection (1) above shall not affect the giving of relief in respect of a payment received by an insurer before 6th April 1999 where—

(*a*) the premium in respect of which the payment is made is a premium under a contract entered into on or after 2nd July 1997 but before 1st August 1997;

(*b*) that contract is one entered into by way of the renewal of an earlier contract;

(*c*) the period of insurance under the earlier contract ended before 2nd July 1997; and

(*d*) if the payment is not itself a payment received before 1st August 1997, the insurer had before 1st August 1997 received an earlier payment in respect of a premium under the renewal contract.

(4) For the purposes of the preceding provisions of this section a contract shall be taken to have been entered into by way of the renewal of an earlier contract only if—

(*a*) it was entered into by way of the renewal of a contract which was an eligible contract for the purposes of section 54 of the Finance Act 1989 when that earlier contract was entered into;

(*b*) the insurer under the earlier contract and the insurer under the contract by which it has been renewed are the same; and

(*c*) the period of insurance under the earlier contract ended immediately before the beginning of the period of insurance under the contract by which it has been renewed.

(5) This section has effect for the year 1997-98 and subsequent years of assessment.

BACKGROUND NOTE

Tax relief for persons paying qualifying private medical insurance premiums insuring those aged 60 and over was first introduced in 1989 (FA 1989 ss 54–57). Relief, originally by deduction, was restricted to the basic rate of tax in 1994 (FA 1989 s 54(3A)–(3C), as inserted by FA 1994 Sch 10 paras 1, 2).

This section abolishes the relief on new contracts as from 2 July 1997 (Budget Day), with certain transitional savings (see below). Relief remains on existing contracts, but the term of qualifying contracts may not exceed one year, so all qualifying contracts will have expired by 31 July 1998. Late premium payments under qualifying contracts will qualify for relief until 6 April 1999.

TRANSITIONAL RELIEF

Payments under existing qualifying contracts (ie contracts already in force on 2 July 1997) continue to qualify for relief. Since no qualifying contract can provide for a period of insurance greater than one year (FA 1989 s 55(2)(*b*)), all such contracts will have lapsed by 1 July 1998.

As an additional transitional measure, where a written proposal for a new contract had been received by or on behalf of the insurer before 2 July 1997, but the contract itself had not yet been made by that date, premiums will qualify for relief provided that—

(*a*) the contract is entered into before 1 August 1997; and

(*b*) the first payment or part payment of a premium under the contract is made before 1 August 1997.

(Sub-s (2).)

Premiums under a contract that is a renewal of an earlier contract will also qualify where—

(*a*) the renewed contract is entered into after 1 July 1997 and before 1 August 1997; and

(*b*) the term of the earlier contract expired before 2 July 1997; and

(*c*) the first payment or part payment of a premium under the contract is made before 1 August 1997.

(Sub-s (3).)

RENEWALS OF A CONTRACT

Subsection (4) defines what is meant by a renewal of an earlier contract for the purposes of the transitional relief. The contract must be with the same insurer, the period of insurance under the renewed contract must begin immediately after the expiry of the period of insurance under the earlier contract and, of course, the earlier contract must have been eligible for relief when it was entered into.

Corporation tax

18   Rates for financial year 1997

(1) The rate at which corporation tax is charged for the financial year 1997 shall be, and shall be deemed always to have been, 31 per cent (and not 33 per cent as provided by section 58 of the Finance Act 1997).

(2) The small companies' rate for that year shall be, and shall be deemed always to have been, 21 per cent (and not 23 per cent as provided by section 59(*a*) of that Act).

(3) All such adjustments shall be made, whether by way of discharge or repayment of tax or otherwise, as may be required in consequence of the provisions of this section.

GENERAL NOTE

This section sets the standard rate of corporation tax for the financial year 1997 (the year ending 31 March 1998) and the small companies rate for that year at 21 per cent. It thus overrides FA 1997 s 58, which set those rates at 33 per cent and 23 per cent respectively.

The lower and upper earnings limits remain at £300,000 and £1,500,000 respectively; and the fraction in the marginal-rate formula remains one-fourtieth (FA 1997 s 59(*b*)).

EXAMPLE

Andromeda Ltd has taxable profits of £800,000 and franked investment income of £100,000 for its accounting period ending 31 March 1998, and has no associated companies. Its corporation tax payable is as follows—

Tax on £800,000 @ 31%	£248,000.00
Marginal relief:	
(£1,500,000−(£800,000+£100,000))×£800,000/£900,000×1/40	13,333.33
Corporation tax payable	£234,666.67

The effective marginal rate of corporation tax on profits falling between the lower and upper earnings limits changes from 35.5 per cent to 33.5 per cent (this computation works only if there is no franked investment income).

Distributions, tax credits etc on and after 2nd July 1997

19 Pension funds no longer entitled to payment of tax credits

(1) In section 231 of the Taxes Act 1988 (tax credits for certain recipients of qualifying distributions)—

(*a*) in subsection (2) (payment of tax credits to companies resident in the United Kingdom) for "Subject to section 241(5)" there shall be substituted "Subject to sections 231A and 241(5)"; and

(*b*) at the beginning of subsection (3) (claims by other persons to set tax credits against income tax liability and to receive payment of any excess of tax credit over that liability) there shall be inserted "Subject to section 231A,".

(2) After section 231 of the Taxes Act 1988 there shall be inserted—

"231A Restrictions on the use of tax credits by pension funds

(1) No claim shall be made under section 231(2) for payment of the amount of a tax credit if or to the extent that the qualifying distribution to which the credit relates is income of a pension fund.

(2) In the case of any pension fund, for any year of assessment the aggregate amount of the tax credits in respect of which claims are made under section 231(3) must not exceed the aggregate amount of the tax credits in respect of the qualifying distributions comprised in the income of the pension fund and brought into charge to tax.

(3) Accordingly, no payment shall be made under section 231(3) in respect of so much of the excess there mentioned as is referable to a tax credit in respect of a qualifying distribution if or to the extent that the qualifying distribution is income of a pension fund.

(4) In this section—

"income", in relation to a pension fund, means income derived from investments or deposits held for the purposes of the pension fund;

"pension fund" means any scheme, fund or other arrangements established and maintained (whether in the United Kingdom or elsewhere) for the purpose of providing pensions, retirement annuities, allowances, lump sums, gratuities or other superannuation benefits (with or without subsidiary benefits);

"scheme" includes any deed, agreement or series of agreements.

(5) For convenience of identification only, the schemes, funds or other arrangements which are "pension funds" for the purposes of this section by virtue of the definition of that expression in subsection (4) above include, in particular, those whose income is, in whole or in part, exempt, or eligible for exemption, from tax under or by virtue of any of the following provisions—

(*a*) section 512(2);
(*b*) section 592(2);
(*c*) section 608(2)(*a*);
(*d*) section 613(4);
(*e*) section 614(2), (3), (4) or (5);
(*f*) section 620(6);
(*g*) section 643(2).

(6) The preceding provisions of this section do not have effect in relation to—

(*a*) claims made in respect of tax credits to which entitlement arises by virtue of section 232(3); or
(*b*) claims made by virtue of arrangements having effect under section 788."

(3) This section has effect in relation to qualifying distributions made on or after 2nd July 1997.

GENERAL NOTE

If an investor receives a dividend from a UK company of £80, the attaching tax credit is £20. Individuals liable to tax at either the lower or basic rate of income tax have no further tax liability. Higher rate taxpayers are entitled to set off the £20 tax credit against their tax liability on the grossed up £100 dividend.

Non-taxpayers, and exempt taxpayers including fully exempt approved pension funds and charities, have been able to recover the £20 tax credit. The largest group of exempt taxpayers are pension schemes and life insurance companies carrying on pension business.

As part of the reform of the corporation tax system announced by the Chancellor of the Exchequer, the recovery of the tax credits attaching to dividends from UK companies will be denied in a two stage process. The first stage is to remove the entitlement of pension funds to recover tax credits in respect of dividends from UK companies made on or after 2 July 1997. The second stage will take effect on 6 April 1999 and will remove the entitlement to payment of tax credits to companies and charities.

A new TA 1988 s 231A is introduced to prevent pension providers established as UK resident companies making a claim to payment of tax credits. It also prevents the ability to set off a tax credit against any other tax liability arising.

20 Losses etc not to be set against surplus franked investment income

(1) No claim shall be made under section 242 or 243 of the Taxes Act 1988 (set off of losses etc against surplus of franked investment income) for any

accounting period beginning on or after 2nd July 1997; and section 244(1) of that Act shall cease to have effect accordingly.

(2) Sections 242(5) and (6) and 243(4) of the Taxes Act 1988 (restoration of loss etc in later accounting period for which there is a surplus of franked payments) shall not have effect where the later accounting period mentioned in section 242(5)(*b*) begins on or after 2nd July 1997.

(3) No amount shall be deducted under paragraph (*a*), or carried forward and deducted under paragraph (*b*), of section 244(2) (deduction of tax credit paid from ACT subsequently available for set off or surrender) for any accounting period beginning on or after 2nd July 1997.

(4) For the purposes of sections 242 and 243 of the Taxes Act 1988, if—

(*a*) a company has a surplus of franked investment income for an accounting period beginning before 2nd July 1997 and ending on or after that date, and
(*b*) that surplus exceeds the surplus of franked investment income which the company would have had for that accounting period had it ended on 1st July 1997,

the surplus shall be treated as reduced by the excess.

(5) Sections 242 to 244 of the Taxes Act 1988 cease to have effect in consequence of, and in accordance with, the foregoing provisions of this section.

(6) In section 237(4) of the Taxes Act 1988 (bonus issue and related tax credit not to be franked investment income for the purposes of sections 241 and 244) for "sections 241 and 244" there shall be substituted "section 241".

(7) Subsection (6) above has effect in accordance with subsection (5) above.

GENERAL NOTE

When a company makes a distribution eg, a dividend of say £80, it pays ACT of 25 per cent (£20) on the distribution. The ACT may be set off against the company's mainstream corporation tax liability, within limits. Any surplus may be carried forward or back and set against future or previous corporation tax liabilities.

If a company receives a dividend, it is not normally liable to corporation tax on that dividend. The company is entitled to a tax credit but normally will use the tax credit to "frank" any dividends paid to its own shareholders. Where a company has trading losses, it has been able to set these losses against its profits (including surplus franked investment income) and claim a repayment of the tax credit.

This section prevents such claims for accounting periods commencing on or after 2 July 1997. Claims for accounting periods straddling 2 July 1997 will be restricted.

21   Estates in administration: distributions to which s 233(1) applies

(1) Section 699A of the Taxes Act 1988 (untaxed sums comprised in the income of the estate) shall be amended as follows.

(2) In subsection (1) (which defines "a relevant amount" by reference to an amount which is or would be paid out of sums to which paragraphs (*a*) and (*b*) apply) after paragraph (*b*) there shall be inserted—

"or out of any sums included in the aggregate income of the estate of the deceased which fall within subsection (1A) below."

(3) After subsection (1) there shall be inserted—

"(1A) A sum falls within this subsection if it is a sum in respect of a distribution to which section 233(1) applies.

(1B) Any reference in this Part to a sum to which subsection (1)(*a*) and (*b*) above applies includes a reference to a sum falling within subsection (1A) above which is included in the aggregate income of the estate of the deceased."

(4) In subsection (4) (rate at which sums are assumed to bear tax) after paragraph (*b*) there shall be inserted "; and

(*c*) in the case of sums falling within subsection (1A) above, at the lower rate."

(5) This section has effect in relation to amounts which a person is deemed by virtue of Part XVI of the Taxes Act 1988 (estates in the course of administration) to receive, or to have a right to receive, on or after 2nd July 1997.

GENERAL NOTE

During the administration period of an estate, personal representatives may receive taxable interest or realise capital gains. If so, they incur a liability to income tax or CGT. The liability of personal representatives to income tax is limited to the lower 20 per cent rate on any savings income or the basic 23 per cent rate on other income such as rent. When personal representatives make payments or transfer assets to beneficiaries, the beneficiaries may be treated as receiving income for tax purposes. The deemed income is treated as paid under deduction of income tax. Beneficiaries who are lower rate or non-taxpayers may be able to claim back some of the tax. Higher rate taxpayers will have further tax to pay.

This section provides for amendments to be made to the treatment of non-qualifying distributions received by personal representatives in the course of estates in administration. Non-qualifying distributions are distributions that do not carry tax credits such as distributions arising on the bonus issue of shares by a company for which no new consideration is received by the company. From 2 July 1997 payments to estate beneficiaries funded out of non-qualifying distributions will be treated as made under deduction of non-repayable tax at the lower rate. This will ensure that the beneficiaries are taxed on the payment from the estate in the same way as if they received the distribution direct.

22   Lloyd's underwriters

(1) In section 171 of the Finance Act 1993 (taxation of profits, and allowance of losses, of non-corporate members) after subsection (2A) there shall be inserted—

"(2B) Section 231(1) of the Taxes Act 1988 (entitlement to tax credit) shall not apply where the distribution there mentioned is a distribution in respect of any asset of a member's premiums trust fund."

(2) In section 219 of the Finance Act 1994 (taxation of profits of corporate

members) at the beginning of subsection (3) there shall be inserted "Subject to subsection (4A) below,".

(3) In subsection (4) of that section (subsection (2) applies in relation to distributions and associated tax credits notwithstanding section 11(2)(*a*) or 208 of the Taxes Act 1988)—

(*a*) for "dividends or other distributions of a company resident in the United Kingdom" there shall be substituted "UK distributions"; and

(*b*) the words "(and any associated tax credits)" shall cease to have effect.

(4) After that subsection there shall be inserted—

"(4A) Notwithstanding anything in section 11(2)(*a*) or 208 of the Taxes Act 1988, UK distributions in respect of any assets of a corporate member which are mentioned in paragraph (*a*) or (*b*) of subsection (3) above—

(*a*) shall be taken into account in computing profits of the corporate member for tax purposes; and

(*b*) shall be so taken into account under Case I of Schedule D (and not under any other Schedule or any other Case of Schedule D).

(4B) Section 231(1) of the Taxes Act 1988 (entitlement to tax credit) shall not apply where the distribution there mentioned is a distribution in respect of any asset of a corporate member's premiums trust fund.

(4C) In this section "UK distributions" means dividends or other distributions of a company resident in the United Kingdom."

(5) In section 20(1) of the Taxes Act 1988, as amended by section 24(10) below, in paragraph 2 of Schedule F (distribution in respect of which a person is entitled to a tax credit treated for the purposes of the Tax Acts, other than section 95(1), as representing income equal to the aggregate of the distribution and the tax credit) after "95(1)" there shall be inserted "of this Act and section 219(4A) of the Finance Act 1994".

(6) In section 231(1) of the Taxes Act 1988 (recipient of distribution made by UK resident company entitled to tax credit subject to sections 247 and 441A) after "441A," there shall be inserted "section 171(2B) of the Finance Act 1993 and section 219(4B) of the Finance Act 1994,".

(7) This section has effect in relation to distributions made on or after 2nd July 1997.

GENERAL NOTE

Profits arising to individual and corporate members of Lloyd's underwriting syndicates are taxed under Case 1 of Schedule D. Profits include income arising from investing premiums received which are held in premiums trust funds until they are required to meet claims. Distributions received by individuals have always been chargeable to income tax in their hands but companies are not normally chargeable to corporation tax on distributions received. It has long been provided for the tax credit related to distribution income from assets of premiums trust funds to be paid into the premiums trust fund and for the total of the distribution itself and the amount paid in respect of the tax credit to be included in the computation of trading profits.

This section ensures that distributions from premiums trust funds no longer attract tax credits in relation to distributions made on or after 2 July 1997. In future the distribution itself will be taxed. It also provides for any other distributions received by corporate members in connection with their underwriting business to be included in trading profits in the same way. Distributions received by individuals in connection with their ancillary trust funds are already included in their trading profits and this will continue.

23 Insurance companies and friendly societies

Schedule 3 to this Act (which makes provision in relation to insurance companies and friendly societies) shall have effect.

GENERAL NOTE

This section gives effect to Sch 3 to this Act, which makes provision in relation to insurance companies and friendly societies. It removes an insurance company's entitlement to payment of tax credits relating to its pension business in respect of dividends and other company distributions made on or after 2 July 1997.

Distributions, tax credits etc: avoidance

24 Taxation of dealers in respect of distributions etc

(1) Section 95 of the Taxes Act 1988 (taxation of dealers in respect of certain qualifying distributions etc) shall be amended in accordance with subsections (2) to (9) below.

(2) For subsection (1) (qualifying distributions to which Schedule 7 to the Finance Act 1997 applies which are received by a dealer, and payments made by a dealer which are representative of such distributions, to be taken into account in computing profits of the dealer) there shall be substituted—

"(1) Where a dealer—

(*a*) receives a relevant distribution, that is to say—

(i) any distribution which is made by a company resident in the United Kingdom ("a UK distribution"), or

(ii) any payment which is representative of a UK distribution, or

(*b*) makes any payment which is representative of a UK distribution,

the distribution or, as the case may be, the payment shall be taken into account in computing the profits of the dealer which are chargeable to tax in accordance with the provisions of this Act applicable to Case I or II of Schedule D."

(3) In subsection (1A) (provisions consequential on subsection (1) where dealer receives qualifying distribution to which Schedule 7 to the Finance Act 1997 applies)—

(*a*) in the words preceding paragraph (*a*), for "qualifying distribution to which Schedule 7 to the Finance Act 1997 applies" there shall be substituted "relevant distribution";

(*b*) paragraph (*b*) (distribution not to be treated for the purposes of sections 246D and 246F as a FID received by the dealer) shall cease to have effect;

(*c*) in paragraph (*c*), for "sections 208 and 234(1)" there shall be substituted "section 208";

(*d*) paragraph (*d*) (which disapplies paragraph 2A(2) of Schedule 23A to the Taxes Act 1988 which is repealed by this section) shall be omitted; and

(*e*) the following paragraph shall be inserted at the appropriate place—

"(*e*) section 11(2)(*a*) shall have effect in relation to that distribution with the omission of the words "(but so that this paragraph shall not include distributions received from companies resident in the United Kingdom)"."

(4) Subsection (1B) (which relates to the application of section 732 and which becomes unnecessary in consequence of the amendments made to that section by section 26 below) shall cease to have effect.

(5) In subsection (2) (meaning of "dealer")—

(*a*) the word "qualifying" shall be omitted in both places where it occurs; and

(*b*) in paragraph (*a*) after "shares" there shall be inserted "or stock".

(6) After subsection (2) there shall be inserted—

"(2A) The reference in subsection (2) above to the profits of a person does not include the profits of that person in respect of insurance business or any category of insurance business."

(7) Subsection (4) (which makes special provision in relation to preference shares) shall cease to have effect.

(8) Subsection (5) (definitions) shall be omitted.

(9) For the side note there shall be substituted "Taxation of dealers in respect of distributions etc."

(10) In section 20(1) of the Taxes Act 1988, in paragraph 2 of Schedule F (distribution in respect of which a person is entitled to a tax credit treated for the purposes of the Tax Acts as representing income equal to the aggregate of the distribution and the tax credit) after "purposes of the Tax Acts" there shall be inserted "(other than section 95(1))".

(11) In section 234 of the Taxes Act 1988 (information relating to distributions) in subsection (1), the words "but subject to section 95(1A)(*c*)" shall be omitted.

(12) In section 246D(1) of the Taxes Act 1988 (individuals entitled to FIDs treated as receiving grossed-up amount) after "that individual shall be treated" there shall be inserted "(except for the purposes of section 95(1))".

(13) In Schedule 23A to the Taxes Act 1988 (manufactured dividends and interest) paragraph 2A(2) (which provides that if the dividend manufacturer is a company not resident in the UK no amount shall be deductible in the case of that company in respect of the manufactured dividend) shall be omitted (and accordingly paragraph 2(3)(*c*) of that Schedule has effect instead).

(14) In Schedule 7 to the Finance Act 1997 (special treatment for certain distributions) in paragraph 2 (distributions treated as FIDs) in sub-paragraph (3)—

(*a*) paragraph (*a*) (subjection to section 95(1A)(*b*)) shall be omitted; and

(*b*) in paragraph (*b*) (subjection to section 247(5B) to (5D)) for "of that Act" there shall be substituted "of the Taxes Act 1988".

(15) This section has effect in relation to—

(*a*) any distribution made on or after 2nd July 1997; and

(*b*) any payment which is representative of such a distribution.

GENERAL NOTE

This section introduces amendments to TA 1988 s 95 which provides for the taxation of dealers in respect of distributions.

Section 95 provides that dealers receiving dividends to which FA 1997 Sch 7 applies (eg special dividends and share buy backs) will be taxable on the receipt of such dividends. Equally, manufactured dividends paid by the dealers which are representative of such dividends will be deductible. Previously such dividends received and paid by UK corporations have not been taxable and allowable respectively.

The Inland Revenue Explanatory Note indicates that "the measures put to an end an anomaly which allowed financial concerns to reduce their taxable trading profits by taking advantage of differences in the tax treatment of dividends and other income arising from trading assets." In the document it cites two examples of such advantages. First, where a financial concern instead of making a loan at interest to a customer takes redeemable preference shares, it will receive tax free dividend income instead of taxable interest. Second, where a dealer in shares buys a share cum div, receives a dividend and sells ex div, it will generate tax-free dividend income and a tax deductible loss.

Section 24(2) introduces a new s 95(1) which determines when s 95 is applicable. For distributions made on or after 2 July 1997 (and payments representative of such dividends) the provision will apply to any dividends received by a dealer and not just those to which FA 1997 Sch 7 applied. As a result, such dividends will be taxable but as noted in the Inland Revenue Explanatory Note "Any tax credit to which the company is entitled in respect of the distribution will not be chargeable to corporation tax but will, like any other tax credit, be available for use in accordance with section 241 TA 1988." Similarly, on manufacturing such a dividend they are entitled to a tax deduction but "they will not be entitled to any such deduction in respect of any ACT paid as a consequence of making a manufactured payment".

Section 95(1A) provides for further amendment to the taxation of such dividends being received by dealers and consequential changes are made to the relevant provisions. First, the revised s 95(1A) will apply to all dividends received by a dealer and not just those within Sch 7. Second, TA 1988 ss 246D–246F, which prevented the distribution received by the dealer from being treated as a FID, are disapplied. Third, TA 1988 s 234(1) will now apply to payments representative of such dividends by the dealer (by reason of sub-s (11)) and there will therefore no longer be an exemption from providing the recipient with a statement of the relevant dividend details.

The remaining changes in s 95(1A) deal with non-UK companies trading in the UK. TA 1988 Sch 23A para 2A(2), which provides that UK branches of non-UK companies are not entitled to a deduction for manufactured dividends on UK equities is repealed in all situations (by sub-s (13)) and therefore its specific disapplication is no longer needed. It is no longer needed as the Inland Revenue Explanatory Note comments "Section 95(1) provides for such payments to be taken into account in computing trading profits". TA 1988 s 11(2), which deals with non-UK companies conducting a trade through a branch or agency, is amended so that such dividends received in the course of that trade will be taxable.

Section 95(1B) currently provides that where dividends are within s 95 that no adjustment is to be made under TA 1988 s 732. Section 732 is an anti-avoidance provision which is designed to counter dividend washing transactions. Section 732 is disapplied by s 26 and so its specific disapplication to trades within s 95 is no longer required.

Subsection (5) provides for amendments to the definition of dealer. Section 95(2) defines dealer as a person who would treat the sale of the shares, on which the qualifying distribution is paid, as giving rise to a Schedule D Case I or II receipt. The amendment removes the requirement for the distribution in question to be a "qualifying distribution" and to ensure that the definition of shares for this purpose includes stock. "Qualifying distribution" is defined by TA 1988 s 14(2) as any "distribution" defined by s 209(2) except those within s 209(2)(c).

Subsection (6) ensures that the profits of an insurance business or any category of insurance business are not considered to be profits of a dealer. Such profits are addressed by s 23 and Sch 3 of the Act.

Subsections (7) and (8) revoke s 95(4) and (5). Section 95(4) previously excluded "fixed rate preference shares" and preference shares issued before 6 April 1982 (or whose terms were substantially settled before this date) from the effect of s 95. Section 95(5) defines fixed rate preference shares.

Subsection (10) provides for amendment of the definition of Schedule F in TA 1988 s 20. In para 2 of Schedule F distributions are defined as including the associated tax credit. Subsection (10) provides that this is not the case for the purposes of s 95. Accordingly the charge under s 95 is restricted to the dividend paid by the company and excludes the associated tax credit.

Subsection (12) provides amendment to TA 1988 s 246D(1). Section 246D(1) provides that an individual receiving a FID is still entitled to a tax credit. The amendment provides that an individual dealer is not entitled to this credit.

Subsection (14) amends FA 1997 Sch 7 para 2(3). Paragraph 2(3) provides that dividends within s 95(1A)(b) will not be treated as a FID and this is to be revoked.

25   Repeal of s 95(5) of the Taxes Act 1988: consequential amendments

(1) In section 246A(9) of the Taxes Act 1988 (which provides that "fixed-rate preference shares" shall be construed in accordance with section 95(5)) for "section 95(5)" there shall be substituted "paragraph 13(6) of Schedule 28B".

(2) In Schedule 28B to the Taxes Act 1988 (venture capital trusts) paragraph 13 (general interpretation) shall be amended in accordance with subsections (3) and (4) below.

(3) In sub-paragraph (5), paragraph (b) (which provides that "fixed-rate preference shares" has the same meaning as in section 95), and the word "and" immediately preceding that paragraph, shall be omitted.

(4) After sub-paragraph (5) there shall be inserted—

    "(6) In this paragraph "fixed-rate preference shares" means shares which—

      (*a*) were issued wholly for new consideration;

      (*b*) do not carry any right either to conversion into shares or securities of any other description or to the acquisition of any additional shares or securities; and

      (*c*) do not carry any right to dividends other than dividends which—

(i) are of a fixed amount or at a fixed rate per cent of the nominal value of the shares, and

(ii) together with any sum paid on redemption, represent no more than a reasonable commercial return on the consideration for which the shares were issued;

and in paragraph (*a*) above "new consideration" has the meaning given by section 254.''

(5) In Schedule 7 to the Finance Act 1997 (special treatment for certain distributions) paragraph 5 (fixed-rate preference shares) shall be amended in accordance with subsections (6) and (7) below.

(6) In sub-paragraph (2) (which defines "fixed-rate preference shares" by reference to section 95 of the Taxes Act 1988)—

(*a*) in paragraph (*a*) for "section 95 of" there shall be substituted "paragraph 13 of Schedule 28B to"; and

(*b*) in paragraph (*b*) for "section 95(5)(*c*)(*i*) of that Act" there shall be substituted "paragraph 13(6)(*c*)(*i*) of that Schedule".

(7) After sub-paragraph (2) there shall be inserted—

"(3) For the purposes of sub-paragraph (2) above, any reference in paragraph 13(6) of Schedule 28B to shares shall be taken as a reference to shares within the meaning of this Schedule."

(8) This section has effect on and after 2nd July 1997.

GENERAL NOTE

This section makes a number of consequential amendments following the removal of TA 1988 s 95(5) by s 24 above.

Subsection 95(5) contained the definition of "fixed rate preference share" for the purposes of s 95 but this definition was imported into a number of other provisions. Section 25 makes provision for the absence of the definition and is effective on and after 2 July 1997.

First, TA 1988 s 246A allows a company paying a dividend to elect for it to be treated as an FID. It contains in sub-s (6) a requirement that the company must not have more than one class of dividends, but in sub-s (9) fixed rate preference shares are ignored for this purpose. The definition of fixed rate preference shares is by reference to s 95(5) and s 25(1) replaces this with the definition in TA 1988 Sch 28B para 13(6).

The definition in para 13 of fixed rate preference share is currently contained in sub-para (5) and is also referenced to s 95(5). This definition is replaced by sub-ss (2)–(4). These insert a new sub-para (6) containing the same definition as was in s 95(5).

Lastly, FA 1997 Sch 7 provides for the treatment of distributions arising from the purchase by a company of its own shares (within para 1(2)) and distributions linked to transactions in securities (within para 1(3)). Dividends on fixed rate preference shares may be within para 1(3) because they are made by virtue of the terms on which the preference shares have been issued and therefore may be considered to be "specified matters" for the purposes of para 1(3) and (4). Paragraph 5 provides that such dividends on fixed rate preference shares are not to be treated as within para 1(3) by that reason alone.

Paragraph 5(2) provides that the definition of fixed rate preference shares is made by reference to s 95(5) and again these references are replaced by Sch 28B para 13(6).

26 Purchase and sale of securities

(1) Section 732 of the Taxes Act 1988 (dealers in securities) shall be amended as follows.

(2) After subsection (1) (dealers in securities: reduction for tax purposes of price paid by the appropriate amount in respect of interest) there shall be inserted—

"(1A) Subsection (1) above shall not apply if the interest receivable by the first buyer falls to be taken into account by virtue of section 95(1) in computing profits of his which are chargeable to tax in accordance with the provisions of this Act applicable to Case I or II of Schedule D."

(3) Subsections (2) and (2A) (exceptions from subsection (1) for certain market makers, recognised clearing houses and members of recognised investment exchanges) shall cease to have effect.

(4) In subsection (4) (exception from subsection (1) for overseas securities bought on a stock exchange outside the United Kingdom if conditions as to computation of profits and non-allowance of credit for foreign tax are satisfied) the words "on a stock exchange outside the United Kingdom" shall be omitted.

(5) For the definition of "overseas securities" in subsection (4) there shall be substituted—

"In this subsection "overseas securities" means securities issued—

(*a*) by a government or public or local authority of a territory outside the United Kingdom; or

(*b*) by any other body of persons not resident in the United Kingdom."

(6) Subsections (5) and (5A) (exceptions from subsection (1) for Eurobonds bought by dealers and for rights in a unit trust scheme where first buyer sells as manager) shall cease to have effect.

(7) Subsections (6) and (7) (definitions for the purposes of subsections (2) and (2A)) shall cease to have effect.

(8) This section has effect where, for the purposes of section 731(2) of the Taxes Act 1988, the interest receivable by the first buyer is paid on or after 2nd July 1997.

General note

This section makes amendments to restrict the application of the anti-dividend washing provisions of TA 1988 s 732.

Sections 731–735 are designed to counter the practice of dividend washing. Dividend washing is achieved by an investor selling a security cum div prior to the receipt of any dividend and receiving the value of the dividend as a capital receipt rather than as income. Counterparties to such trades will be in the opposite position acquiring a security with a high tax basis at the expense of receiving dividend income. Those which would be willing to undertake such a trade with a "dividend washer" are therefore limited, however there are certain counterparties such as dealers in securities for whom this consequence need not be disadvantageous. For a dealer the acquisition and the disposal of the security would be taken into account in computing trading profits.

Sections 731–735 impose a charge on the counterparty to such trades to provide a fiscal disincentive to their participation in such trades with dividend washers.

Dealers in securities are now subject to tax on UK dividend income received by reason of TA 1988 s 95 as amended by s 24 above. Accordingly, there is no longer a need for these provisions to apply in respect of dividends on UK equities. Section 26 therefore provides that s 732(1) will not apply where the dividend has been taxed as a result of s 95(1). However, the changes do go further than required solely by this change.

As a result of this exemption the existing exemptions available to market makers and members of recognised investment exchanges contained in s 732(2) and (2A) are no longer needed. Section 26(3) therefore deletes them together with sub-ss (6) and (7) which contained associated definitions.

It had been intended to reform the exemption as a result of the reform of UK equity trading on the London Stock Exchange. The Inland Revenue Explanatory Note states that "the secondary legislation intended to give effect to this exclusion which was referred to in the Inland Revenue's Press Release of 5 December 1996: 'Financial markets: Tax rules on share trading' will not now be necessary. The existing secondary legislation, at SI 1992/568 and SI 1995/2050 which defines the classes of dealer excluded from the provisions of s 732(1) will cease to have effect on 2 July 1997."

Section 732 also applies in respect of overseas securities. Subsection (4) contains an exemption from the penal effects of the section provided that the securities are brought on an overseas stock exchange in the ordinary course of the securities dealer's trade, provided that the income is brought into charge to tax and a foreign tax credit is not claimed. Subsection (4) removes the requirement for the overseas stock to be brought on an overseas exchange, although the other conditions continue. The definition of overseas security is also amended to include securities issued by public or local authorities outside the UK and the scope to include securities of the Republic of Ireland.

Subsection (6) removes two other exemptions. First, it repeals s 732(5) which provided an exemption in respect of Eurobonds for Eurobond dealers. Second, it repeals s 732(5A) which provided an exemption for managers of unit trust schemes in respect of units in that scheme.

These changes are effective for interest and dividends paid on or after 2 July 1997.

27 Payments to companies under section 687 of the Taxes Act 1988

(1) After section 687 of the Taxes Act 1988 (payments under discretionary trusts) there shall be inserted—

"687A Payments to companies under section 687

(1) This section applies where—

    (*a*) trustees make a payment to a company;
    (*b*) section 687 applies to the payment; and
    (*c*) the company is chargeable to corporation tax and does not fall within subsection (2) below.

(2) A company falls within this subsection if it is—

    (*a*) a charity, as defined in section 506(1);
    (*b*) a body mentioned in section 507 (heritage bodies); or

(*c*) an Association of a description specified in section 508 (scientific research organisations).

(3) Where this section applies—

(*a*) none of the following provisions, namely—

(i) section 7(2),
(ii) section 11(3),
(iii) paragraph 5(1) of Schedule 16,

shall apply in the case of the payment;

(*b*) the payment shall be left out of account in calculating the profits of the company for the purposes of corporation tax; and
(*c*) no repayment shall be made of the amount treated under section 687(2) as income tax paid by the company in the case of the payment.

(4) If the company is not resident in the United Kingdom, this section applies only in relation to so much (if any) of the payment as is comprised in the company's chargeable profits for the purposes of corporation tax.''

(2) This section has effect in relation to payments made by trustees to companies on or after 2nd July 1997.

GENERAL NOTE

Section 27 introduces TA 1988 s 687A to prevent possible abuse by companies seeking to receive their UK dividend income through trusts.

Section 687A applies to payments by trustees to a company chargeable to corporation tax where s 687 applies. Companies falling with s 687A(2) are excluded from its provisions and these are charities within TA 1988 s 506(1), heritage bodies within TA 1988 s 507 and scientific research organisations within TA 1988 s 508.

Section 687 applies where trustees exercise their discretion and make income payments to beneficiaries. The payments are treated as a net amount with a tax credit based upon the rate for trusts for the year, currently 34 per cent. The recipient is entitled to a credit and the income is treated as an annual payment. The trustees are assessable for the tax, but are able to set off certain tax suffered against this tax liability and this includes the tax credits on UK dividends. The concern was therefore raised in the Inland Revenue Explanatory Note that "without action companies could arrange for their dividend income to be paid to them via a trust and in effect continue to enjoy the benefit of the tax credits".

Where s 687A applies, sub-s (3) provides that the payment shall not be chargeable to tax. Further, it provides that no repayment of the income tax on the annual payment received by a company shall be made, the income tax may not be used to set off against its corporation tax liability under TA 1988 s 7(1) (or s 11(3) for non-UK resident companies), nor against other income tax liabilities under TA 1988 Sch 16 para 5(1).

Where the company is not UK resident, sub-s (4) provides that the section only applies in respect of a payment within charge to UK tax, through a UK branch or agency.

The section is effective for payments made by trustees on or after 2 July 1997.

28 Arrangements to pass on value of tax credit

(1) After section 231A of the Taxes Act 1988 (which is inserted by section 19 of this Act) there shall be inserted—

"231B Consequences of certain arrangements to pass on the value of a tax credit

(1) This section applies in any case where—

(a) a person ("A") is entitled to a tax credit in respect of a qualifying distribution;

(b) arrangements subsist such that another person ("B") obtains, whether directly or indirectly, a payment representing any of the value of the tax credit;

(c) the arrangements (whether or not made directly between A and B) were entered into for an unallowable purpose; and

(d) the condition in subsection (2) below is satisfied.

(2) The condition is that if B had been the person entitled to the tax credit and the qualifying distribution to which it relates, and had received the distribution when it was made, then—

(a) B would not have been entitled to obtain any payment under section 231(2) or (3) in respect of the tax credit; and

(b) if B is a company, B could not have used the income consisting of the distribution to frank a distribution actually made in the accounting period in which it would have received the distribution to which the tax credit relates.

(3) This section does not apply if and to the extent that any other provision of the Tax Acts has the effect of cancelling or reducing the tax advantage which would otherwise be obtained by virtue of the arrangements.

(4) Where this section applies—

(a) no claim shall be made under section 231(2) for payment of the amount of the tax credit;

(b) no claim shall be made under section 231(3) or 441A(7) in respect of the tax credit;

(c) the income consisting of the distribution in respect of which A is entitled to the tax credit shall not be regarded for the purposes of section 241 as franked investment income; and

(d) no claim shall be made under section 35 of the Finance (No 2) Act 1997 (transitional relief) for payment of an amount determined by reference to that distribution.

(5) For the purposes of this section, the question whether any arrangements were entered into for an "unallowable purpose" shall be determined in accordance with subsections (6) and (7) below.

(6) Arrangements are entered into for an unallowable purpose if the purposes for which at least one person is a party to the arrangements include a purpose which is not amongst the business or other commercial purposes of that person.

(7) Where one of the purposes for which a person enters into any

33

arrangements is the purpose of securing that that person or another obtains a tax advantage, that purpose shall be regarded as a business or other commercial purpose of the person only if it is neither the main purpose, nor one of the main purposes, for which the person enters into the arrangements.

(8) Any reference in this section to a person obtaining a tax advantage includes a reference to a person obtaining a payment representing any of the value of a tax credit in circumstances where, had the person obtaining the payment been entitled to the tax credit and the qualifying distribution to which it relates, that person—

> (*a*) would not have been entitled to obtain any payment under section 231(2) or (3) in respect of the tax credit; and
> (*b*) if that person is a company, could not have used the income consisting of the distribution to frank a distribution actually made in the accounting period in which it would have received the distribution to which the tax credit relates.

(9) If an amount representing any of the value of a tax credit to which a person is entitled is applied at the direction of, or otherwise in favour of, some other person (whether by way of set off or otherwise), the case shall be treated for the purposes of this section as one where that other person obtains a payment representing any of the value of the tax credit.

(10) In determining for the purposes of subsections (2)(*b*) and (8)(*b*) above whether a company could have used the income consisting of the distribution in question to frank a distribution of the company, the company shall be taken to use its actual franked investment income to frank distributions before using the income consisting of the distribution in question.

(11) References in this section to using franked investment income to frank a distribution of a company have the same meaning as in Chapter V of Part VI.

(12) In this section—

> "arrangements" means arrangements of any kind, whether in writing or not (and includes a series of arrangements, whether or not between the same parties);
> "business or other commercial purposes" includes the efficient management of investments;
> "franked investment income" has the same meaning as in Chapter V of Part VI and references to income consisting of a distribution shall be construed accordingly;
> "tax advantage" has the same meaning as in Chapter I of Part XVII."

(2) This section has effect in relation to distributions made on or after 2nd July 1997.

GENERAL NOTE

This section introduces a new TA 1988 s 231B designed to counter arrangements to pass on the value of credits.

Section 231B deals with a person "A" who is entitled to a tax credit in respect of a qualifying distribution. If arrangements subsist with another person "B" such that B obtains (directly or indirectly) a payment representing any of the value of the credit and the arrangements (direct or indirect) were entered into for an "unallowable purpose" and certain conditions in sub-s (2) are satisfied, then the section applies.

For this purpose arrangements mean arrangements of any kind whether in writing or not and include a series of arrangements regardless of whether they are between the same parties.

The conditions in sub-s (2) are that if B had received the tax credit in question it would not have been able to obtain credit under TA 1988 s 231(2) or (3) or could not have used it to frank a distribution made in the same accounting period in which it would have been received. (For this purpose the company shall be taken to use its actual franked investment income to frank its payments in the accounting period first.) Section 231(2) allows a refund of the credit where a UK resident company receiving it is wholly exempt from tax or is exempt on all but trading income, or where the distribution is specifically exempt otherwise than by reason of TA 1988 s 208. Section 231(3) allows a refund where the distribution is received by a person other than a UK resident company to the extent that it exceeds his income tax liability for the year, subject to certain conditions.

A purpose is "unallowable" if it falls within sub-ss (6) and (7). A purpose is "unallowable" if the purposes of one person to the arrangements include a purpose which is not amongst its business or other commercial purposes (including the efficient management of investments). Where one of the purposes in question is to secure a tax advantage for that person or another, then the person will not be regarded as having a business or other commercial purpose unless that purpose is not the main, or one of the main, purposes for which the person entered into the arrangements.

For this purpose a tax advantage has the same meanings as in s 709(1). Further, a tax advantage is obtained where a person obtains a payment representing any of the value of the credit in circumstances where had that person been entitled to the tax credit and the qualifying distribution, sub-s (2) would have applied.

Where the value of a credit is applied by the person entitled to it at the direction (or otherwise in favour) of another person that other person is treated as having received the benefit of the payment representing any value of the credit.

The Inland Revenue Explanatory Note comments that "the purpose of the clause is to prevent tax avoidance by which a person obtains a benefit of tax credits on UK dividend income to which he or she would not be entitled if he or she had received the UK dividend income directly. It is not intended to preclude bona fide commercial transactions such as stock lending and repo arrangements, or hedging as part of efficient management of investments".

Where s 231B applies, claims to obtain value for the tax credit are denied. First, no claim can be made under TA 1988 s 231(2) or (3). Second, no claim may be made under s 441A(7) which deals with insurance companies' overseas life assurance funds. Third, the income is not to be treated as franked investment income for the purposes of calculating a company's ACT liability on its qualifying distributions under TA 1988 s 241. Fourthly, no claim is allowed under F(No 2)A 1997 s 35.

Section 231B is effective for distributions made on or after 2 July 1997, but is disapplied to the extent that other provisions cancel or reduce the tax benefit obtained.

29 Unauthorised unit trusts

(1) Where a qualifying distribution—

(*a*) is made on or after 2nd July 1997 but before 6th April 1999 by a company resident in the United Kingdom, and

(*b*) falls to be regarded by virtue of subsection (2) of section 469 of the Taxes Act 1988 (unit trusts other than authorised unit trusts) as income of the trustees of a unit trust scheme to which that section applies, and

(*c*) is not a foreign income dividend and does not fall to be regarded by virtue of any provision of the Tax Acts apart from this section as a foreign income dividend arising to the trustees,

the trustees shall be treated for all purposes of the Tax Acts (apart from this section) as if the qualifying distribution were a foreign income dividend.

(2) Subsection (1) above shall not apply—

(*a*) if the unit trust scheme is a common investment fund established under section 42 of the Administration of Justice Act 1982; or

(*b*) if, apart from section 469(2) of the Taxes Act 1988, the whole of the qualifying distribution would fall to be regarded as income of section 505 bodies.

(3) In this section—

"foreign income dividend" shall be construed in accordance with Chapter VA of Part VI of the Taxes Act 1988;

"section 505 body" means—

(*a*) a charity, as defined in section 506(1) of the Taxes Act 1988;

(*b*) a body mentioned in section 507 (heritage bodies) of that Act; or

(*c*) an Association of a description specified in section 508 of that Act (scientific research organisations).

GENERAL NOTE

This section provides that qualifying distributions received by unauthorised unit trusts will be treated as FIDs where the relevant conditions are met.

The clause applies to dividends made on or after 2 July 1997 but before 6 April 1999, at which time the remaining entitlements to have tax credits paid will be substantially removed (see s 30). It applies where the qualifying distribution is treated as the income of the trustees by TA 1988 s 469(2) rather than the unit holders and the distribution is not otherwise treated as an FID.

An FID is as defined in TA 1988 Chapter VA Part VI.

The effect is that the trustees will have no entitlement to a tax credit in respect of the distribution in question and will not be treated as having paid any tax on the distribution.

There are exceptions for common investment funds established under the Administration of Justice Act 1982 s 42 and for unauthorised unit trusts where the whole of the income would otherwise fall to be regarded as income of a TA 1988 "section 505 body", that is a charity (under TA 1988 s 506(1)), heritage body (TA 1988 s 507) or scientific research organisation (TA 1988 s 508).

In the Inland Revenue Explanatory Note the purpose of the provision is explained as "to prevent pension funds circumventing the provisions in clause 19 by investing in UK equities through the medium of unauthorised unit trusts". The trustees of unauthorised unit trusts are taxed on the income received. Payments to unit holders are treated as annual payments made net of basic rate tax, which tax exempt organisations are entitled to be repaid. The concern is that by channeling dividends on which they could not receive tax credits through an unauthorised unit trust, pension funds would then be able to obtain a refund of the income tax associated with the annual payment distributed by the trustees, which the tax credit has been used to frank.

Distributions, tax credits etc in and after 1999-00

30   Tax credits

(1) Section 231 of the Taxes Act 1988 (tax credits for certain recipients of qualifying distributions) shall be amended in accordance with subsections (2) to (7) below.

(2) In subsection (1) (recipient of certain distributions to be entitled to tax credit equal to proportion of distribution corresponding to rate of ACT in force)—

(a) after "where" there shall be inserted ", in any year of assessment for which income tax is charged,"; and
(b) for "the rate of advance corporation tax in force for the financial year in which" there shall be substituted "the tax credit fraction in force when."

(3) After subsection (1) there shall be inserted—

"(1A) The tax credit fraction is one-ninth."

(4) Subsection (2) (payment of tax credit to company resident in UK) shall cease to have effect.

(5) In subsection (3) (which includes provision for payment of excess of tax credit over income tax liability to person not being a company resident in the UK)—

(a) for "Subject to section 231A," there shall be substituted "Subject to subsection (3AA) below,"; and
(b) the words "and subject to subsections (3A) and (3D) below and section 231A where the credit exceeds that income tax, to have the excess paid to him" shall cease to have effect.

(6) After subsection (3) there shall be inserted—

"(3AA) For any year of assessment, the aggregate amount of the tax credits in respect of which claims are made under subsection (3) above by any person must not exceed the aggregate amount of the tax credits in respect of such qualifying distributions (if any) as are brought into charge to tax in the case of that person."

(7) In consequence of subsection (5) above, subsections (3A) to (3D) shall cease to have effect.

(8) Section 231A of the Taxes Act 1988 (which is superseded by the foregoing provisions of this section) shall cease to have effect.

(9) The amendments made by subsections (5) and (6) above do not affect the entitlement of a person who is not resident in the United Kingdom to payment

in respect of a tax credit by virtue of arrangements having effect under section 788 of the Taxes Act 1988 (relief by agreement with other countries).

(10) Where—

(*a*) arrangements having effect by virtue of section 788 of the Taxes Act 1988 confer on a person not resident in the United Kingdom the right to a tax credit under section 231 of the Taxes Act 1988 in respect of a dividend of a company resident in the United Kingdom, and

(*b*) the arrangements contain provision for permitting—

(i) tax to be charged or deducted, or

(ii) a reduction in the amount of the tax credit that is paid to be made,

by reference to the aggregate of the dividend and the tax credit, and

(*c*) the amount of that tax or that reduction exceeds the amount of the tax credit,

that provision shall only have the effect of reducing to nil the amount of the payment to which the person is entitled in respect of the tax credit.

(11) This section has effect in relation to distributions made on or after 6th April 1999.

BACKGROUND NOTE

Under the imputation system of corporation tax, the recipient of a dividend or other distribution from a UK company is entitled to a tax credit to take account of the fact that the company has paid corporation tax on the profit out of which the distribution has been paid. At present the rate of the credit is 20 per cent of the total of the distribution and the credit, ie 25 per cent of the distribution. Where the recipient is an individual the credit can be set against the income tax liability on the distribution or, if the credit exceeds the total income tax liability, the difference can be repaid. A body of persons (such as a charity or a pension fund) which is entitled to exemption from tax can claim repayment of the credit and a UK company which is entitled to relief in respect of losses may be able to claim repayment.

GENERAL NOTE

This section amends the treatment of tax credits for distributions paid after 5 April 1999 (sub-s (11)). The effect is twofold: first, the rate of credit is reduced to 10 per cent and second, the right to repayment of credit (where it exceeds the total tax liability) is withdrawn. (The right to repayment of credit is withdrawn from 2 July 1997 for pension providers and most other UK companies by sub-ss (19), (20)).

RATE OF CREDIT

The rate is no longer to be determined by reference to the rate of advance corporation tax but by reference to the "tax credit fraction" in force at the time when the distribution is paid (sub-s (2)). The tax credit fraction is initially fixed at one-ninth (sub-s (3)). This is equivalent to a tax credit rate of 10 per cent of the sum of the distribution and the credit. For example, if a company pays a dividend of £9,000 on 1 June 1999, the credit will be £1,000 (one-ninth of £9,000) which is 10 per cent of £10,000 (£9,000 plus credit £1,000). This bears no relation to the ACT (£2,250) payable by the company, based on the lower income tax rate of 20 per cent.

CANCELLATION OF RIGHT TO REPAYMENT OF CREDIT

A UK company which is exempt from tax (or only taxable on trading income) will no longer be able to claim payment of tax credits on distributions received (sub-s (4) repealing TA 1988 s 231(2)). There is transitional relief for charitable companies (see s 35 below).

A person, other than a company, resident in the UK will only be entitled to claim relief for tax credits on distributions received so far as they are charged to tax. This means that charities and individuals who have allowances to set against income in the form of distributions will not be able to claim payment of the credits (sub-ss (5)–(8) amending TA 1988 s 231 and repealing TA 1988 s 231A which was inserted by s 19 above).

The removal of the right to payment of tax credits on distributions does not affect persons not resident in the UK who are entitled to payment under the terms of a double taxation agreement (sub-s (9)). Where such an agreement provides for a reduction of the amount of tax credit by reference to the grossed up amount of the distribution, there are circumstances in which the reduction may exceed the amount of the credit; in such a case the only effect is to reduce to nil the amount of the payment in respect of the credit (sub-s (10)).

31   Rates of tax applicable to Schedule F income etc

(1) Section 1A of the Taxes Act 1988 (application of lower rate to income from savings and distributions) shall be amended in accordance with subsections (2) to (4) below.

(2) In subsection (1) (certain savings and distribution income to be charged at the lower rate to the exclusion of basic rate) for "lower rate" there shall be substituted "rate applicable in accordance with subsection (1A) below".

(3) After subsection (1) there shall be inserted—

"(1A) The rate applicable in accordance with this subsection is—

(*a*) in the case of income chargeable under Schedule F, the Schedule F ordinary rate;
(*b*) in the case of equivalent foreign income falling within subsection (3)(*b*) below and chargeable under Case V of Schedule D, the Schedule F ordinary rate; and
(*c*) in the case of any other income, the lower rate."

(4) For subsection (5) (income to which section 1A applies to be treated as the highest part of a person's income) there shall be substituted—

"(5) For the purposes of subsection (1)(*b*) above and any other provisions of the Income Tax Acts—

(*a*) so much of any person's income as comprises income to which this section applies shall be treated as the highest part of his income; and
(*b*) so much of that part as consists of—

(i) income chargeable under Schedule F (if any), and
(ii) equivalent foreign income falling within subsection (3)(*b*) above and chargeable under Case V of Schedule D (if any),

shall be treated as the highest part of that part."

(5) After section 1A of the Taxes Act 1988 there shall be inserted—

"1B   Rates of tax applicable to Schedule F income etc

(1) In the case of so much of an individual's income which consists of—

(*a*) income chargeable under Schedule F (if any), and
(*b*) equivalent foreign income falling within section 1A(3)(*b*) and chargeable under Case V of Schedule D (if any),

as is income falling within section 1(2)(*b*), income tax shall, by virtue of this subsection, be charged at the Schedule F upper rate, instead of at the rate otherwise applicable to it in accordance with section 1(2)(*b*).

(2) In relation to any year of assessment for which income tax is charged—

(*a*) the Schedule F ordinary rate is 10 per cent, and
(*b*) the Schedule F upper rate is 32.5 per cent,

or, in either case, such other rate as Parliament may determine."

(6) This section has effect in relation to distributions made on or after 6th April 1999.

BACKGROUND NOTE

Income from savings is at present charged to income tax at the lower rate of 20 per cent on the gross amount of the income, except where the recipient is an individual liable at the higher rate of 40 per cent. In the case of a dividend or other distribution paid by a UK company, the gross amount means the amount of the distribution plus the corresponding amount of tax credit. The recipient is entitled to set off the amount of the credit against the liability, which means that where an individual is liable at the lower or basic rate, the credit will satisfy the liability and, where he is liable at the higher rate, he will pay at 20 per cent on the gross amount.

GENERAL NOTE

This section amends TA 1988 s 1A by introducing two further rates of income tax for 1999–2000 (sub-s (6)) which apply to dividends and other distributions by UK companies and to equivalent foreign income.

THE NEW RATES

Income chargeable under Schedule F and equivalent foreign income will no longer be charged at the lower rate of 20 per cent but at the Schedule F ordinary rate (sub-ss (2), (3)). This rate is fixed at 10 per cent (TA 1988 s 1B(2)(*a*) inserted by sub-s (5)). Where such income is chargeable at a rate in excess of the basic rate, it will be charged at the Schedule F upper rate which is fixed at 32.5 per cent (TA 1988 s 1B(2)(*b*) inserted by sub-s (5)). These rates may be amended by Parliament.

TA 1988 s 1A(5) provides that any savings income shall (for the purposes of tax at a rate in excess of the basic rate) be treated as the highest part of the income of an individual. This is to be extended by providing that any income chargeable under Schedule F or equivalent foreign income will be treated as the top slice of the savings income (sub-s (4)).

From 6 April 1999 there will be five rates of income tax—

(*a*) the Schedule F ordinary rate (10 per cent);
(*b*) the lower rate (20 per cent);
(*c*) the basic rate (23 per cent);

(*d*) the Schedule F upper rate (32.5 per cent);
(*e*) the higher rate (40 per cent).

EXAMPLE

A UK company pays dividends of £800 on 1 June 1998 and 1 June 1999 to an individual who is liable at a rate in excess of the basic rate. His liability will be—

		1998–99		*1999–2000*
		£		£
Dividend		800		800
Tax credit		200	1/9th	88.89
		1,000		888.89
Tax charge	40%	400	32.5%	288.89
Less tax credit		200		88.89
Tax payable		200		200.00

32   Trusts

(1) Section 686 of the Taxes Act 1988 (income arising to trustees which is to be chargeable at the rate applicable to trusts) shall be amended as follows.

(2) In subsection (1) (income to which the section applies to be chargeable at the rate applicable to trusts instead of at the basic rate or, in accordance with section 1A, the lower rate)—

(*a*) for "at the rate applicable to trusts" there shall be substituted "at the rate applicable in accordance with subsection (1AA) below"; and
(*b*) after "at the lower rate" there shall be inserted "or the Schedule F ordinary rate".

(3) After subsection (1) there shall be inserted—

"(1AA) The rate applicable in accordance with this subsection is—

(*a*) in the case of so much of any income to which this section applies as is Schedule F type income, the Schedule F trust rate; and
(*b*) in the case of any other income to which this section applies, the rate applicable to trusts."

(4) In subsection (1A) (the rate applicable to trusts etc) for the words from the beginning to "Parliament may determine" there shall be substituted—

"(1A) In relation to any year of assessment for which income tax is charged—

(*a*) the Schedule F trust rate shall be 25 per cent, and
(*b*) the rate applicable to trusts shall be 34 per cent,

or, in either case, such other rate as Parliament may determine."

(5) In subsection (1A), so as to make the words following "as Parliament may determine" into a separate paragraph, for the words "and, for the purposes of assessments" there shall be substituted—

"For the purposes of assessments".

(6) In subsection (2AA) (income treated by s 689B as applied in defraying trustees' expenses to be taxed at the rate that would apply apart from s 686,

instead of the rate applicable to trusts) after "instead of the rate applicable to trusts" there shall be inserted "or the Schedule F trust rate (as the case may be)".

(7) Before subsection (6) there shall be inserted—

"(5A) In this section "Schedule F type income", in relation to trustees, means—

(*a*) income chargeable under Schedule F;

(*b*) income to which section 1A applies by virtue of its being equivalent foreign income falling within subsection (3)(*b*) of that section and chargeable under Case V of Schedule D;

(*c*) a qualifying distribution whose amount or value is determined in accordance with section 233(1A);

(*d*) a non-qualifying distribution, within the meaning of section 233(1B);

(*e*) income treated as arising to the trustees by virtue of section 249(6)(*b*);

(*f*) income treated as received by the trustees by virtue of section 421(1)(*a*);

(*g*) any amount which, by virtue of section 686A, is treated for the purposes of the Tax Acts as if it were income to which this section applies."

(8) For the sidenote there shall be substituted "Accumulation and discretionary trusts: special rates of tax."

(9) After section 686 of the Taxes Act 1988 there shall be inserted—

"686A   Certain distributions to be treated as income to which section 686 applies

(1) This section applies where—

(*a*) a qualifying distribution is made to trustees;

(*b*) the trustees are not the trustees of a unit trust scheme; and

(*c*) the qualifying distribution falls within subsection (2) below.

(2) A qualifying distribution falls within this subsection if it is a payment made by a company—

(*a*) on the redemption, repayment or purchase of its own shares; or

(*b*) on the purchase of rights to acquire its own shares.

(3) The relevant part of the distribution shall be treated for the purposes of the Tax Acts as if it were income to which section 686 applies.

(4) In subsection (3) above the reference to the relevant part of the distribution is a reference to so much (if any) of the distribution as—

(*a*) is not income falling within paragraph (*a*) of section 686(2);

(*b*) does not fall to be treated for the purposes of the Income Tax Acts as income of a settlor;

(*c*) is not income arising under a trust established for charitable purposes; and

(*d*) is not income from investments, deposits or other property held for any such purposes as are mentioned in sub-paragraph (*i*) or (ii) of section 686(2)(*c*).

(5) Subsection (6) of section 686 shall apply for the purposes of this section as it applies for the purposes of that section.''

(10) The amendment made by subsection (5) above has effect on and after 6th April 1999.

(11) The other amendments made by this section have effect in relation to distributions made on or after 6th April 1999.

GENERAL NOTE

Section 32 is a provision for discretionary trust income after 5 April 1999 which is consequential on the changes made by ss 30 and 31 to the tax treatment of company distributions after that date.

TA 1988 s 686 imposes a special rate of income tax on discretionary trust income, the rate of tax falling between the higher personal rate of income tax and the basic rate. Discretionary trust income for this purpose means income which is distributable at the discretion of the trustees, or subject to a trust to accumulate it, which is neither income of anyone other than the trustees before being distributed nor deemed to be the income of the settlor (eg under TA 1988 s 660A), and which is not charity or pension fund income: see TA 1988 s 686(2). At present such income is taxed at 34 per cent, in contrast to the lower rate of income tax of 20 per cent, the basic rate of 23 per cent and the higher rate of 40 per cent. However, after tax at the rate for discretionary trust income has been paid it can be available as a credit under TA 1988 s 687 if and when the income is distributed to a beneficiary and taxable as his income.

As explained above, s 30 of this Act will reduce the tax credit for company distributions to the equivalent of 10 per cent of the aggregate of the distribution and tax credit, and s 31 will reduce individual taxpayers' liability to income tax on them to 10 per cent or a higher rate of 32.5 per cent, both sections applying to distributions after 5 April 1999. Accordingly, it is appropriate to amend TA 1988 s 686 so that the rate of income tax paid on discretionary trust income which consists of company distributions made after that date is also reduced. This is done by s 32, and it reduces the rate of tax on such income to 25 per cent, which is a reduction by 9 per cent in contrast to the 10 per cent decrease in the rate for individuals. There is consequential amendment to TA 1988 s 687 made by Sch 4 para 15 of this Act (see below).

DETAILS OF THE PROVISIONS

Subsections (2) and (3) amend TA 1988 s 686 to define a ''Schedule F trust rate'' and a ''rate applicable to trusts'', the former being that for dividends and other ''Schedule F type income'' and the latter being for other discretionary trust income. Subsection (4) adds sub-s (1A) to s 686 which specifies the two rates as 34 per cent and 24 per cent respectively, but which of course may be amended by FA 1998 or FA 1999 before these provisions start to operate. Subsection (5) is a verbal amendment consequent on sub-s (4), and sub-s (6) is a verbal amendment consequent on there being two rates instead of one under s 686.

Subsection (7) inserts a new TA 1988 s 686(5A) which will define the types of discretionary trust income to which the lower 25 per cent rate will apply. Paragraph (*a*), income chargeable under Schedule F, refers to all dividends and other distributions of a company resident in the UK (TA 1988 s 20). Paragraph (*b*) refers to income from companies not resident in the UK which would be taxed under Schedule F if the company were resident in the UK (see TA 1988 s 1A(2)(*c*), (3)(*b*)). Paragraph (*c*) refers to distributions from UK companies to trusts where the trustees are resident outside the UK. Paragraph (*d*) refers to the issue to trustees of redeemable share capital otherwise than for full consideration. Paragraph (*e*) refers to stock dividends which are chargeable to income tax, and para (*f*) refers to taxable write-offs of loans to participators in a close company. Paragraph (*g*) refers to the redemption by a company of redeemable capital or the purchase by a company of its own shares: see below.

Subsection (8) amends the sidenote to s 686 to reflect more closely what it will deal with in its amended form. Subsection (9) inserts a new TA 1988 s 686A to treat as income chargeable under s 686 any "qualifying distribution" which is the purchase or redemption by a company of its own shares or rights to acquire its own shares. There are exceptions for unit trusts, charities, pension funds and distributions taxed as the settlor's income (s 686A(1)(*b*), (4)). Income taxed by virtue of the new TA 1988 s 686A will be chargeable to the Schedule F trust rate appropriate to dividends etc, ie 25 per cent unless and until the provisions contained in s 32(4) are amended: see the new TA 1988 s 686(5A)(*g*) to be added by s 32(7). A "qualifying distribution" is, broadly, any distribution of cash or other assets out of a company to holders of shares or securities, other than the issue of redeemable capital (see TA 1988 ss 14(2) and 209(2)). The new TA 1988 s 686A will replace FA 1997 Sch 7 para 3, which is in similar terms, but which will be repealed from 1999–2000 because of other changes to corporate taxation.

33   Estates of deceased persons in administration

(1) For section 698A of the Taxes Act 1988 (taxation at the lower rate of the income of beneficiaries) there shall be substituted—

"698A   Taxation of income of beneficiaries at lower rate or at rates applicable to Schedule F income

(1) Subject to subsection (3) below, in so far as any income of any person is treated under this Part as having borne income tax at the lower rate, section 1A shall have effect as if that income were income to which that section applies otherwise than by virtue of the income being income chargeable under Schedule F.

(2) Subject to subsection (3) below, in so far as any income of any person is treated under this Part as having borne income tax at the Schedule F ordinary rate, that income shall be treated as if it were income chargeable under Schedule F.

(3) Subsections (1) and (2) above shall not apply to income paid indirectly through a trustee and treated by virtue of section 698(3) as having borne income tax at the lower rate or the Schedule F ordinary rate; but, subject to section 686(1), section 1A shall have effect as if the payment made to the trustee were income of the trustee—

(*a*) to which section 1A applies by virtue of the income being chargeable under Schedule F, in the case of income treated as having borne tax at the Schedule F ordinary rate; and

(*b*) to which section 1A applies otherwise than by virtue of the income being chargeable under Schedule F, in any other case."

(2) Section 699A of the Taxes Act 1988 (untaxed sums comprised in the income of the estate) shall be amended in accordance with subsections (3) to (6) below.

(3) In subsection (1A) (which is inserted by section 21 of this Act and describes sums to which subsection (1)(*a*) and (*b*) of s 699A is deemed to apply) after "if it is a sum in respect of" there shall be inserted—

"(*a*) a distribution chargeable under Schedule F; or
(*b*) ".

(4) In subsection (2) (determination whether any amount is a relevant amount) in paragraph (*b*) (application of the assumption in section 701(3A)(*b*)) for "assumption" there shall be substituted "assumptions".

(5) In subsection (4) (rate at which sums are assumed to bear tax) in paragraphs (*a*) and (*c*) for "lower rate" there shall be substituted "Schedule F ordinary rate".

(6) In subsection (6) (income represented by a relevant amount to be treated as not brought into charge to tax for the purposes of ss 348 and 349(1)) at the end there shall be added "except to the extent that the relevant amount is or would be paid out of sums in respect of a distribution chargeable under Schedule F".

(7) In section 701 of the Taxes Act 1988 (interpretation of Part XVI) subsection (3A)(which defines the "applicable rate" as basic rate or lower rate, according to the rate at which the income of the residue out of which the payment to the beneficiary is made bears tax) shall be amended in accordance with subsections (8) and (9) below.

(8) For the words "or the lower rate", in both places where they occur, there shall be substituted ", the lower rate or the Schedule F ordinary rate".

(9) In paragraph (*b*) (assumption that payments are made out of income bearing tax at the basic rate before income bearing tax at the lower rate)—

(*a*) after "it shall be assumed" there shall be inserted "(*i*)";
(*b*) after "lower rate" there shall be inserted "or the Schedule F ordinary rate"; and
(*c*) at the end of the paragraph there shall be added

"; and
(ii) that payments are to be made out of income bearing tax at the lower rate before they are made out of income bearing tax at the Schedule F ordinary rate."

(10) The amendment made by subsection (3) above has effect in relation to distributions made on or after 6th April 1999.

(11) The amendments made by subsections (1) and (4) to (9) above have effect for the year 1999–00 and subsequent years of assessment.

GENERAL NOTE

This is again a provision consequential on the changes made to the taxation of company distributions by ss 30 and 31, and which has effect for the tax year 1999–2000 and subsequently. The income of the residuary estate of a deceased person is taxed as the income of the personal representatives and when that income is distributed to the beneficiaries interested in residue, or the administration comes to an end, it is then taxed as those beneficiaries' income under TA 1988 ss 695–702 (credit being given for tax already paid). Section 33 of this Act will ensure that where income of the personal representatives consists of company distributions made after 5 April 1999 which are chargeable to income tax at the "Schedule F ordinary rate", provisionally put under this Act at 10 per cent (see s 31 above), that income when distributed to beneficiaries will be treated as income subject to the same tax rate, and the beneficiary will not be able to claim a repayment of that tax.

TA 1988 ss 695(4) (in relation to limited interests in residue) and 696(4) (in relation to absolute interests in residue) treat income treated as received by a beneficiary as having been received subject to deduction of tax at the "applicable rate", which at the moment is either the basic rate or the lower rate for savings income according to the rate at which the personal representatives' income from which the income comes has borne tax (see TA 1988 s 701(3A)). TA 1988 s 701(3A) will be amended by sub-ss (8) and (9) of this section so that the applicable rate will be the basic rate, lower rate, or Schedule F ordinary rate according to the rate at which the relevant income of the personal representatives was taxed. The rules for identifying the income of beneficiaries with that of the personal representatives for this purpose will be modified so that income is treated as paid first out of the income taxed at the basic rate, second out of that taxed at the lower rate and last of all out of income taxed at the Schedule F ordinary rate.

The tax credit is not the end of the story, as further provision is needed so that income of beneficiaries treated as made out of income taxed at the lower rate or Schedule F ordinary rate is treated as income liable to income tax at those respective rates in the hands of the beneficiary. This will be achieved by the replacement TA 1988 s 698A(1) and (2), provided by sub-s (1) of this section. Where the income of the estate is distributed to or treated as the income of trustees of a discretionary trust TA 1988 s 686 will still apply to it, but the trustees will be treated under the replacement TA 1988 s 698A(3) as receiving income taxable at the lower rate or the Schedule F ordinary rate according to its source. This is to ensure that the additional income tax payable under TA 1988 s 686 is that which is appropriate to the nature of the underlying income.

Subsections (2)–(6) of this section amend TA 1988 s 699A, which at the moment treats payments to beneficiaries out of certain kinds of deemed income of a deceased person's estate as having borne basic or lower rate income tax, but without the beneficiary being able to recover the tax if his personal circumstances cause the income not to be taxable in his hands. The amendments made by sub-ss (2)–(6) will, from 1999–2000 on, extend this treatment to company distributions chargeable to income tax under Schedule F, so that the beneficiaries who receive distributions of such income from an estate will be credited with the Schedule F tax already paid but will not be able to obtain a repayment of it.

34 Tax credits and taxation of distributions: miscellaneous provisions

Schedule 4 to this Act (which contains provisions relating to tax credits and the taxation of distributions) shall have effect.

GENERAL NOTE

This section introduces Sch 4 which contains consequential amendments to the Taxes Acts to take account of the new treatment of tax credits on company distributions etc.

35 Transitional relief for charities etc

(1) In any case where—

(*a*) a qualifying distribution is made on or after 6th April 1999 and before 6th April 2004 by a company resident in the United Kingdom; and
(*b*) the recipient of the distribution is a section 505 body; and
(*c*) if the section 505 body falls within neither paragraph (*b*) nor paragraph (*c*) of subsection (3) below, entitlement to exemption from tax by virtue of subsection (1)(*c*)(iii) of section 505 of the Taxes Act 1988 (charities) in respect of the distribution is not prevented by anything in that section,

the section 505 body, on a claim made under this section to the Board, shall be entitled to be paid by the Board out of money provided by Parliament an amount determined in accordance with subsection (2) below.

(2) The amount referred to in subsection (1) above is an amount equal to—

(*a*) 21 per cent of the amount or value of the distribution if the distribution is made on or after 6th April 1999 and before 6th April 2000;
(*b*) 17 per cent of that amount or value if the distribution is made on or after 6th April 2000 and before 6th April 2001;
(*c*) 13 per cent of that amount or value if the distribution is made on or after 6th April 2001 and before 6th April 2002;
(*d*) 8 per cent of that amount or value if the distribution is made on or after 6th April 2002 and before 6th April 2003;
(*e*) 4 per cent of that amount or value if the distribution is made on or after 6th April 2003 and before 6th April 2004.

(3) For the purposes of this section each of the following is a section 505 body—

(*a*) any charity (as defined in section 506(1) of the Taxes Act 1988);
(*b*) each of the bodies mentioned in section 507 of that Act (heritage bodies);
(*c*) any Association of a description specified in section 508 of that Act (scientific research organisations).

(4) Schedule 5 to this Act shall have effect to remove or restrict entitlement to payment under this section in certain circumstances.

(5) For the purposes of Chapter I of Part XVII of the Taxes Act 1988 (cancellation of tax advantages) payment of an amount under this section shall be treated as repayment of tax.

(6) Any entitlement of a section 505 body to a payment under subsection (1) above shall be subject to a power of the Board to determine (whether before or after any payment is made) that, having regard to the operation in relation to the distribution in question of section 703 of the Taxes Act 1988 (cancellation of tax advantages) that body is to be treated as if it had had no entitlement to that payment or to so much of it as they may determine.

(7) No claim may be made under this section later than two years after the end of the chargeable period of the section 505 body in which the distribution is made.

(8) An appeal may be brought against any decision of the Board under this

section or under Schedule 5 by giving written notice to the Board within thirty days of receipt of written notice of the decision.

(9) An appeal under this section shall lie to the Special Commissioners, and the provisions of the Taxes Management Act 1970 relating to appeals under the Tax Acts shall apply to an appeal under this section as they apply to those appeals.

(10) Any payment of an amount under this section shall be treated for the purposes of section 252 of the Taxes Act 1988 (rectification of excessive set-off etc of ACT or tax credit) as a payment of tax credit.

GENERAL NOTE

Charities will no longer be able to claim payment of tax credits on company distributions paid after 5 April 1999 (s 30 above). To mitigate the effect of this loss of tax credit, the Revenue will make compensation payments over a five-year period on a (reducing) proportion of the amount of the distributions.

BODIES QUALIFYING FOR PAYMENTS

Claims may be made (sub-ss (1), (3)) by—

(*a*) a charity as defined in TA 1988 s 506 which is entitled to exemption from tax on Schedule F income;
(*b*) a heritage body within TA 1988 s 507; and
(*c*) a scientific research organisation within TA 1988 s 508.

PAYMENTS WHICH MAY BE CLAIMED

Such a body may make a claim in respect of qualifying distributions made by a UK company after 5 April 1999 and before 6 April 2004 (sub-s (1)). The claim must be made within two years of the end of the chargeable period in which the distribution is made (sub-s (7)). Payment will be made by the Revenue out of public funds.

Where anti-avoidance provisions are involved, the payment will be treated as a repayment of tax, but the Revenue may in such circumstances refuse to make all or part of the payment claimed (sub-ss (5), (6)). An appeal may be made to the Special Commissioners against a Revenue decision (sub-ss (8), (9)).

If an excess payment has been made, it may be recovered as if it were a payment of tax credit (sub-s (10)).

The amounts which may be claimed are a proportion of the amount or value of the distribution, depending on the tax year in which the distribution is made (sub-s (2))—

1999–2000	21 per cent
2000–01	17 per cent
2001–02	13 per cent
2002–03	8 per cent
2003–04	4 per cent

36   Foreign income dividends

(1) No election shall be made under section 246A of the Taxes Act 1988 (election for dividend to be treated as foreign income dividend) in respect of any distributions made on or after 6th April 1999.

(2) No amount shall be shown as available for distribution as foreign income dividends in the distribution accounts of an authorised unit trust for a distribution period the distribution date for which falls on or after 6th April 1999.

(3) No distribution made on or after 6th April 1999 shall be treated as a foreign income dividend by virtue of paragraph 2(1) of Schedule 7 to the Finance Act 1997 (Tax Acts to have effect as if qualifying distributions to which Schedule 7 applies were foreign income dividends).

(4) Schedule 6 to this Act (which makes provision for and in connection with the repeal of provisions relating to foreign income dividends) shall have effect.

(5) In subsection (2) above, "distribution accounts", "distribution date" and "distribution period" shall be construed in accordance with section 468H of the Taxes Act 1988 (interpretation of sections 468I to 468R of that Act).

BACKGROUND NOTE

This section and Sch 6 effectively repeal the Foreign Income Dividend ("FID") provisions contained in TA 1988 with effect from 6 April 1999.

The FID regime was introduced in 1994 to ameliorate the position of UK resident companies which derive a significant proportion of their profits overseas and as a result often find that a significant proportion of the ACT paid on dividends is surplus. Essentially this arises from the interaction of the ACT regime and the UK's double tax relief provisions which have the effect of crediting overseas tax against the mainstream corporation tax ("MCT") otherwise due on the profits remitted to the UK. However, if the overseas tax is high enough this means that (unless the companies in question have adequate ACT capacity in respect of other profits) there is no or little remaining MCT against which the ACT can be offset.

The FID regime, albeit complex in implementation, was designed to enable companies in such a position to recover part or all of the ACT which was surplus and could be shown to be attributable to the distribution of overseas profits. The International Headquarters Company ("IHC") regime is a variant of the FID regime enabling UK companies which satisfy the various definitions of IHC not to account for ACT at all and then recover it, instead only having a residual corporation tax liability which, had they not been IHCs, would have equalled the ACT accounted for under the basic FID regime which was irrecoverable.

Since announcement of the abolition of FIDs, several well-known companies which are not IHCs have expressed considerable concern over the abolition of the regime and indicated the possibility of their needing to emigrate tax residence from the UK (to avoid the surplus ACT cost which would result from removal of the FID regime). There are indications that a modified IHC regime may be introduced for companies which derive a significant proportion of their profits outside the UK and not just IHCs as the Treasury Notes on Clauses suggested.

GENERAL NOTE

Sub-section (1) provides that a company cannot elect to treat a dividend as an FID if the dividend is paid on or after 6 April 1999. Accordingly, in respect of distributions from authorised unit trusts ("AUTs") made after 5 April 1999 sub-s (2) provides no such distribution can be treated as a FID (essentially to enable the "FID tax credit" to frank the ACT otherwise due on a FID distribution from the AUT).

Sub-section (3) disapplies the deeming as FIDs by virtue of para 2(1) of FA 1997 Sch 7 certain dividends and other distributions made by companies after 5 April 1999: transactions affected included payments made in connection with share repurchases and dividends sufficiently linked to "transactions in securities".

Sub-section (4) introduces Sch 6 to the Act which gives effect to the repeal of the FID legislation and sub-s (5) introduces by cross-reference to TA 1988 s 468H definitions relevant to sub-s (2).

Gilt-edged securities

37 Interest to be paid gross

(1) The Taxes Act 1988 shall be amended as follows.

(2) In section 50 (Treasury direction for payment of public revenue dividends without deduction of tax), before subsection (1) there shall be inserted the following subsection—

"(A1) The interest on registered gilt-edged securities (whenever issued and whatever the terms on which they were issued) shall be paid without deduction of income tax."

(3) In that section—

(a) in subsection (1), after "following securities" there shall be inserted "in so far as they are not gilt-edged securities";
(b) in subsection (2), after "by virtue of" there shall be inserted "subsection (A1) above or of";
(c) in subsection (3), for "to which subsection (1) above applied" there shall be substituted "the interest on which is to be paid without deduction of income tax"; and
(d) in subsections (4) and (5), for the words "two months", in each place where they occur, there shall be substituted "one month".

(4) In subsection (7) of that section, after "requires" there shall be inserted the following definition—

""gilt-edged securities" means any securities which—

(a) are gilt-edged securities for the purposes of the 1992 Act; or
(b) will be such securities on the making of any order under paragraph 1 of Schedule 9 to that Act the making of which is anticipated in the prospectus under which they were issued,".

(5) Section 51A (interest on gilt-edged securities held under authorised arrangements to be paid without deduction of tax) shall cease to have effect.

(6) In section 51B (periodic accounting for tax on interest on gilt-edged securities), for subsection (5) there shall be substituted the following subsections—

"(5) In this section "relevant gilt-edged securities" means securities of one of the following descriptions—

(a) gilt-edged securities issued before 6th April 1998 other than those in relation to which a direction under section 50(1) was given before that date;

(b) gilt-edged securities issued on or after that date in relation to which the Treasury have given a direction that they may be subjected to periodic accounting;

and in this subsection "gilt-edged securities" has the same meaning as in section 50.

(5A) Regulations under this section shall not apply to a payment of interest on any relevant gilt-edged securities if that payment is made at any time after the Treasury have given a direction that those securities are to be exempted from periodic accounting."

(7) In sections 722A(5) and 730C(9), and in paragraph 3A(2)(a) of Schedule 23A, (which all define "gilt-edged securities" by reference to section 51A of the Taxes Act 1988), for "51A" there shall be substituted, in each case, "50".

(8) Subject to subsections (9) to (13) below, this section has effect in relation to payments of interest falling due on or after 6th April 1998.

(9) Subsection (3)(d) above has effect in relation to applications made and notices given at any time on or after the day on which this Act is passed.

(10) Where—

(a) any person holds any gilt-edged securities in relation to which a direction was given under section 50(1) of the Taxes Act 1988 at any time before 6th April 1998, and

(b) that person at any time before that date made an application under section 50(2) of that Act with respect to those securities,

that application (unless withdrawn) shall have effect in relation to any interest on those securities to which section 50(A1) of that Act applies as it previously had effect in relation to any interest on those securities to which that direction applied.

(11) Sections 50, 51B and 118D(4) of the Taxes Act 1988 shall have effect in relation to any gilt-edged securities issued before 6th April 1998 which—

(a) are securities the interest on which, if paid immediately before that date, would have fallen to be paid after deduction of income tax, and

(b) are registered within the meaning of section 50 of that Act but are not securities in relation to which any direction under section 50 of that Act was given before that date,

as if the appropriate person had so made an application under section 50(2) of that Act as to enable that application to take effect in relation to payments of interest made on or after that date.

(12) In subsection (11) above "the appropriate person" means—

(a) in the case of securities transferred before 6th April 1998 but after the time when the balance was struck for a dividend on them falling due on or after that date, the person who held the securities at the time when the balance was so struck;

(b) in any other case, the person holding the securities in question immediately before 6th April 1998.

(13) Section 50(5) of the Taxes Act 1988 shall have effect in relation to an application treated as made by virtue of subsection (11) above as if a notice

withdrawing that application was capable of being given at any time on or after the passing of this Act.

GENERAL NOTE

This section provides authority for interest on gilt-edged securities to be paid gross and makes a number of consequential amendments.

These changes have effect for interest falling due on or after 6 April 1998, subject to sub-ss (9)–(13), which are noted below.

UK government securities (gilts) have generally paid interest under deduction of tax, but there are exemptions. TA 1988 s 50 contains exemptions for specific registered securities, eg war loan stock. TA 1988 s 51A was introduced in FA 1995 as part of the introduction of a gilt repo market and allows interest on gilts held under authorised arrangements, the STAR account procedures, to be paid gross. In this later case certain recipients are liable to account for tax on the receipt of the income under TA 1988 s 51B and the associated regulations. This self withholding applies to companies.

Section 37(2) inserts a new subsection (A1) in s 50 and provides that all registered gilt-edged securities are to be paid gross. Gilt-edged securities are defined for the purpose of s 50 by reference to TCGA 1992 Sch 9 Part I using the same definition as is currently contained in s 51A(7).

Section 50(2)–(6) currently allows holders of securities within s 50 to request that tax is withheld and this is amended so that it applies to the new sub-s (A1). There is currently a two month notice period for such an election to be effective and for any withdrawal of the notice to take effect. This period is reduced to one month as a result of the shortening of the ex div period for gilts. Sub-section (9) provides that this change will be effective for applications and notices after the passing of this Act. Sub-section (10) also provides that existing applications under s 50(2) for net payment will continue to be applicable for the new s 50(A1).

There will accordingly be no need for the STAR account arrangements contained in s 51A and it is repealed by sub-s (5). However, as this section contains the definition of "gilt-edged securities" which is referred to in a number of other sections, consequential changes are needed.

In s 51B, which provides for the self withholding noted above, the definition in sub-s (5) is replaced. The new reference is to the definition now contained in s 50. It is also made clear that the self withholding does not apply to gilts issued before 6 April 1998 where the Treasury had directed gross payment should be made under s 50, but does apply to securities issued after this date where the Treasury have made a direction that self withholding should apply. A new sub-s (5A) provides that the self withholding ceases to apply if the Treasury make a direction exempting the security in question.

Sub-section (7) amends the definition of gilt-edged securities from s 51A to s 50 in each of TA 1988 s 722A(5) and s 730C(9), which sections provide for the taxation of stripped gilt-edged securities, and TA 1988 Sch 23A para 3A(2)(*a*), which allows manufactured payments in respect of interest on gilts to be made gross.

Sub-section (11) relates to interest paid to an "appropriate person" in respect of registered gilt-edged securities within s 50, issued before 6 April 1998, which would previously have been paid net as no Treasury direction for gross payment was made. "Appropriate person" for this purpose is the person holding the securities at 6 April 1998, or the holder on the ex div date for interest with an ex date before but payment on or after 6 April. Where sub-s (11) applies, ss 50, 51B and 118D(4) (see s 38) apply as if an application under s 50(2) for net payment had been made. Thus those receiving interest on or after 6 April 1998, that would have been paid net, are to be treated as if the holder had made application for net payment to continue. Such holders may under sub-s (13) apply to have this deemed application for net payment to be withdrawn at anytime after the passing of the Act.

38   Paying and collecting agents

(1) Chapter VIIA of Part IV of the Taxes Act 1988 (paying and collecting agents) shall be amended as follows.

(2) Section 118A (interpretation of Chapter) shall become subsection (1) of that section and, in paragraph (*k*) of that subsection (meaning of "international organisation"), for "has the meaning given by section 51A(8)" there shall be substituted "means an organisation of which two or more sovereign powers, or the governments of two or more sovereign powers, are members".

(3) After that subsection there shall be inserted the following subsection—

"(2) If, in any proceedings, any question arises whether a person is an international organisation for the purposes of this Chapter, a certificate issued by or under the authority of the Secretary of State stating any fact relevant to that question shall be conclusive evidence of that fact."

(4) In section 118D(4) (payments of interest payable without deduction of tax not to be chargeable payments), after "by virtue of" there shall be inserted "section 50(A1) or of".

(5) In subsection (3) of section 118G (United Kingdom public revenue dividends excluded from being chargeable payments)—

(*a*) paragraphs (*b*) and (*d*) to (f) shall be omitted; and
(*b*) for paragraph (*c*) there shall be substituted the following paragraph—

"(ca)   they are payable in respect of a FOTRA security (within the meaning of section 154 of the Finance Act 1996) which—

(i) is not registered (within the meaning of section 50 of this Act); and
(ii) is, for the time being, beneficially owned by a person who is not ordinarily resident in the United Kingdom."

(6) In section 118G(7), for paragraphs (*a*) and (*b*) there shall be substituted "foreign dividends on foreign holdings held by a nominee approved for the purposes of this subsection".

(7) Section 118G(8) and (10) shall cease to have effect.

(8) This section has effect in relation to payments falling due on or after 6th April 1998.

GENERAL NOTE

This section introduces amendments to the paying and collecting agent withholding provisions in respect of gilts following the changes in s 37 above.

Section 38(2) and (3) insert a definition of "international organisation" in TA 1988 s 118A. Presently the definition is made by reference to TA 1988 s 51A(8), but this has now been deleted by s 37 above. The definition inserted corresponds to that in s 51A(8) at present.

Section 118D determines whether items are "chargeable payments" or "chargeable receipts" for the purposes of the Chapter. Section 118D(4) currently provides that interest on gilts which are payable gross by reason of s 50(1) are not chargeable payments (unless a request for net payment has been made under s 50(2)). Sub-section (4) provides that this exclusion from the definition of chargeable payments is similarly extended to gross payments of interest on gilts under s 50(A1) as introduced by s 37 above.

Section 118G provides that certain "relevant payments" will not be "chargeable payments" and "relevant receipts" will not be "chargeable receipts". Section 118G(3) provides such an exception for certain UK public revenue dividends. Sub-section (5) deletes the categories contained in s 118G(3), which are no longer needed as a result of the changes to s 50. These are first (*b*), which deals with gross payments under s 51A, second (*d*)—income of charities eligible for relief under s 505(1)(*c*), third—(*e*) income exempt by reason of various pension reliefs and, finally, (*f*)—the category of such other person as may be prescribed.

Sub-section (5) also amends the exception in s 118G(3) in respect of FOTRA securities. FOTRA securities are defined by FA 1996 s 154(8) as securities issued under F(No 2)A 1931 s 22(1) (which permits issues on terms that allows investors not ordinarily resident in the UK to be exempted from income tax) and three and a half per cent War Loan 1952 Or After issued under F(No 2)A 1915 s 47. Sub-section (5) introduces a new s 118G(3)(*ca*) to replace the existing (*c*) to extend the exemption to FOTRA stocks in bearer form (which would not otherwise fall within the definition in s 50 which is for registered stock only).

Section 118G(7) provides that paying agents do not treat, inter alia, UK public revenue dividends held by approved nominees as chargeable payments. This exclusion is deleted. Section 118G(8) and (10) provide similar relief in respect of such securities held in similar circumstances where treaty relief is applicable. These too are deleted.

The changes are effective for payments falling due on or after 6 April 1998.

Relief for losses etc

39 Carry-back of trading losses

(1) Section 393A of the Taxes Act 1988 (set-off of trading losses against profits of previous three years) shall be amended in accordance with subsections (2) to (6) below.

(2) In subsection (2) (three year carry-back period), for "is the period of three years" there shall be substituted "is (subject to subsection (2A) below) the period of twelve months".

(3) After that subsection there shall be inserted the following subsections—

"(2A) This section shall have effect in relation to any loss to which this subsection applies as if, in subsection (2) above, the words "three years" were substituted for the words "twelve months".

(2B) Where a company ceases to carry on a trade at any time, subsection (2A) above applies to the following—

(*a*) the whole of any loss incurred in that trade by that company in an accounting period beginning twelve months or less before that time; and

(*b*) the part of any loss incurred in that trade by that company in an accounting period ending, but not beginning, in that twelve months which is proportionate to the part of that accounting period falling within that twelve months.

(2C) Where—

(*a*) a loss is incurred by a company in a ring fence trade carried on by that company, and

(*b*) the accounting period in which the loss is incurred is an accounting period for which an allowance under section 62A of the 1990 Act (demolition costs relating to offshore machinery or plant) is made to that company,

subsection (2A) above applies to so much of the amount of that loss not falling within subsection (2B) above as does not exceed the amount of that allowance.''

(4) In subsection (7) (application of section 393(9))—

(*a*) at the beginning there shall be inserted "Subject to subsection (7A) below,''; and

(*b*) for "the accounting period in which the cessation occurs" there shall be substituted "an accounting period ending with the cessation, or ending at any time in the twelve months immediately preceding the cessation,''.

(5) After that subsection there shall be inserted the following subsection—

''(7A) For the purposes of this section where—

(*a*) subsection (7) above has effect for computing the loss for any accounting period, and

(*b*) that accounting period is one beginning before the beginning of the twelve months mentioned in that subsection,

the part of that loss that is not the part falling within subsection (2B)(*b*) above shall be treated as reduced (without any corresponding increase in the part of the loss that does fall within subsection (2B)(*b*) above) by an amount equal to so much of the aggregate of the charges on income treated as expenses by virtue of subsection (7) above as is proportionate to the part of the accounting period that does not fall within those twelve months.''

(6) After subsection (11) there shall be inserted the following subsection—

''(12) In this section "ring fence trade" has the same meaning as in section 62A of the 1990 Act.''

(7) In section 343 of that Act (company reconstructions without a change of ownership), the following subsection shall be inserted after subsection (4)—

''(4A) Subsection (2A) of section 393A shall not apply to any loss which (but for this subsection) would fall within subsection (2B) of that section by virtue of the predecessor's ceasing to carry on the trade, and subsection (7) of that section shall not apply for the computation of any such loss.''

(8) Subject to subsection (9) below, this section applies to any loss incurred in an accounting period ending on or after 2nd July 1997.

(9) Where a loss in any trade is incurred by a company in an accounting period ending on or after 2nd July 1997 but beginning before that date, section 393A of the Taxes Act 1988 shall have effect as if subsection (2A) of that section

applied to the pre-commencement part of any amount of that loss to which that subsection would not apply apart from this subsection.

(10) In subsection (9) above "the pre-commencement part", in relation to the amount of the whole or any part of a loss in an accounting period, means the part of that amount which, on an apportionment in accordance with subsection (11) or, as the case may be, (12) below, is attributable to the part of that accounting period falling before 2nd July 1997.

(11) Except in a case where subsection (12) below applies, an apportionment for the purposes of subsection (10) above shall be made on a time basis according to the respective lengths of the part of the accounting period falling before 2nd July 1997 and the remainder of that accounting period.

(12) Where the circumstances of a particular case are such that the making of an apportionment on the time basis mentioned in subsection (11) above would work in a manner that would be unjust or unreasonable in relation to any person, the apportionment shall be made instead (to the extent only that is necessary in order to avoid injustice and unreasonableness) in such other manner as may be just and reasonable.

BACKGROUND NOTE

From April 1991, the period for which trading losses could be carried back and offset against prior profits was increased from one to three years in response to a severe economic downturn in the UK. The economic rationale underlying the relief is that a longer carry-back period has the potential to accelerate or even increase the recovery of tax paid in earlier, profitable, years by a company suffering current year losses. It appears that, following the recent change of Government, the new Chancellor's view of the current economic climate is that it has improved sufficiently to remove the need for such a relief and he has accordingly returned to a one year carry-back.

Subsections (1)–(6) provide amendments to TA 1988 s 393A (losses set off against profits of the same, or an earlier, accounting period), while sub-s (7) amends TA 1988 s 343 (company reconstructions without a change of ownership) and sub-ss (8)–(12) provide commencement and transitional rules.

AMENDMENTS TO TA 1988 s 393A

Subsection (2) is amended to substitute a reference to "twelve months" for all references to "three years". This effectively leaves in place the existing machinery of loss carry-back and merely reduces the period for which the trading loss incurred in a current accounting period can be carried back. However, this is to be subject to new sub-s (2A).

New subsection (2A) retains the existing three year carry-back period in two cases which are dealt with in sub-ss (2B) and (2C). Subsection (2B) retains the three year carry-back for losses incurred in a period of twelve months prior to the date on which a trade has ceased; while sub-s (2C) retains it in respect of a loss incurred by a company claiming special capital allowances which are only given to petroleum extracting companies (under CAA 1990 s 62A).

The loss incurred on cessation by the oil extracting company has to be looked at in two ways: the part consisting of the capital allowances, which is dealt with under sub-s (2C) and the balance of the loss (if any), which is dealt with under sub-s (2B). The capital allowances in question are 100 per cent allowances claimed in respect of expenditure on the demolition of offshore oil rigs in the North Sea, in compliance with an abandonment programme on the partial or complete closing down of an oil field (as that is defined in the Oil Taxation Act 1975). The separately taxed trade of petroleum extraction is referred to as a "ring fenced trade" (see new sub-s (12), itself referring back to CAA 1990 s 62A).

Where there is more than one accounting period ending in the 12 months prior to the cessation of a trade, new sub-s (2B)(*b*) provides that the losses incurred in the accounting period which commenced more than 12 months prior to the date of cessation are to be apportioned, with only the proportion relating to the later part being eligible for three year carry-back (the earlier part will only be eligible for one year carry-back). This treatment is also applied to trade charges treated as expenses of a trade (by virtue of TA 1988 s 393(9)). Subsection (7), with the insertion of a new sub-s (7A), provides apportionment rules. Trade charges are to be apportioned on the same basis as the other losses of the period (ie, generally on a time apportionment basis).

AMENDMENTS TO TA 1988 S 343

Where there has been a transfer of a trade or a part of a trade from a predecessor company (which then ceases to carry it on) to a successor company, without there having been a change of ownership as defined in the section, generally losses and other reliefs of the predecessor company are carried forward and may be utilised by the successor company. New sub-s (4A) ensures that for the purposes of the cessation rules of TA 1988 s 393A(2B), such a transfer does not qualify as a cessation which would otherwise enable losses to be carried back for a maximum of three years.

COMMENCEMENT AND TRANSITIONAL PROVISIONS—SUB-SS (8)–(12)

The amended TA 1988 s 393A is to apply to losses incurred in accounting periods ending on or after 2 July 1997. However, where such an accounting period spans 2 July 1997, the losses incurred in that accounting period are to be split and the pre-commencement (ie pre-2 July 1997) part of the losses will continue to be eligible for a maximum three year carry back (the balance of the losses only being eligible to be carried back for a maximum of 12 months).

Generally, in such cases, the losses will be apportioned on a time basis but, where time apportionment would work in a manner which would be unjust or unreasonable, the basis adopted can be some other method which will produce a just and reasonable result.

40   Carry-back of loan relationship deficits

(1) Chapter II of Part IV of the Finance Act 1996 (loan relationships) shall be amended as follows.

(2) In paragraph 3(7) of Schedule 8 (permitted period of three years for carry-back of deficits), for "three years" and "three year" there shall be substituted, in each case, "twelve months".

(3) In sub-paragraph (3) of paragraph 4 of Schedule 11 (carry-back of deficit by insurance companies)—

  (*a*) for paragraph (*a*) there shall be substituted the following paragraph—

  "(*a*) carried back to accounting periods falling wholly or partly within the period of twelve months immediately preceding the deficit period; and";
  and

(*b*) in paragraph (*b*), for "those periods" there shall be substituted "up to three such periods".

(4) In sub-paragraph (5) of that paragraph (mechanism for carry-back in the case of insurance companies), for "the three accounting periods preceding the deficit period" there shall be substituted "accounting periods falling wholly or partly within the period of twelve months mentioned in sub-paragraph (3)(*a*) above".

(5) In sub-paragraph (8) of that paragraph (which defines the set-off periods), in each of paragraphs (*b*) and (*c*), for "immediately preceding" there shall be substituted "(if any) which falls wholly or partly within the period of twelve months mentioned in sub-paragraph (3)(*a*) above and immediately precedes".

(6) In sub-paragraph (9) of that paragraph (adjusted amount of a company's eligible profit), after "is" there shall be inserted "(subject to sub-paragraph (9A) below)"; and after that sub-paragraph there shall be inserted the following sub-paragraph—

"(9A) Where a set-off period falls only partly within the period of twelve months mentioned in sub-paragraph (3)(*a*) above, the adjusted amount of a company's eligible profit for that period shall be taken to be confined to the part of the amount computed under sub-paragraph (9) above which is proportionate to the part of the set-off period that falls within that period of twelve months."

(7) Subject to subsection (8) below, this section has effect in relation to any deficit for a deficit period ending on or after 2nd July 1997.

(8) Paragraph 3 of Schedule 8 to the Finance Act 1996 shall have effect in relation to any deficit for a deficit period beginning before but ending on or after 2nd July 1997 as if the permitted period in relation to the pre-commencement part of the deficit were the period beginning with 1st April 1996 and ending immediately before the beginning of the deficit period.

(9) Where for the purposes of paragraph 23 of Schedule 15 to the Finance Act 1996 (transitional provision in connection with the carrying back of exchange losses) there is a relievable amount for an accounting period ending on or after 2nd July 1997, that paragraph shall have effect, except in relation to any pre-commencement part of that amount, as if, in section 131(10)(*b*) of the Finance Act 1993 (the permitted period) as applied by that paragraph, the words "twelve months" were substituted for the words "three years".

(10) In this section "pre-commencement part", in relation to the deficit for any deficit period or the relievable amount for any accounting period, means the part (if any) of that deficit or relievable amount which, on an apportionment in accordance with subsection (11) or, as the case may be, (12) below, is attributable to such part (if any) of that period as falls before 2nd July 1997.

(11) Except in a case where subsection (12) below applies, an apportionment for the purposes of subsection (10) above shall be made on a time basis according to the respective lengths of the part of the deficit period or, as the case may be, accounting period falling before 2nd July 1997 and the remainder of that period.

(12) Where the circumstances of a particular case are such that the making of

an apportionment on the time basis mentioned in subsection (11) above would work in a manner that would be unjust or unreasonable in relation to any person, the apportionment shall be made instead (to the extent only that is necessary in order to avoid injustice and unreasonableness) in such other manner as may be just and reasonable.

BACKGROUND NOTE

FA 1996 introduced comprehensive legislation to govern the taxation treatment of interest (both payable and receivable) and the other "fruits" of debt instruments and loans (collectively referred to in the legislation as "loan relationships"). This followed on from the earlier overhaul of the legislation affecting foreign exchange gains and the results of transactions in financial instruments in FA 1993 and FA 1994.

The amendments in s 39 deal with loss carry-back rules which, inter alia, affect interest payable and other losses arising out of a loan relationship, trade charges, foreign exchange losses and losses arising on transactions in financial instruments, in the context of a trade taxed under Schedule D Case I. The amendments to the legislation contained in s 40 are required to align the carry-back rules for non-trade deficits (ie all such losses, other than those eligible for relief in the context of a trade) with those for trading losses.

The rules contained in FA 1996 for the utilisation of non-trade deficits against profits from various sources effectively combine the non-trade deficits arising out of loan relationships with losses arising from foreign exchange and transactions in financial instruments.

Subsection (2) amends FA 1996 Sch 8 (dealing with non-trade deficits generally) and sub-ss (3)–(6) amend FA 1996 Sch 11 (dealing with the position for insurance companies carrying on life or capital redemption business). Subsections (7)–(12) provide commencement and transitional rules.

AMENDMENTS TO FA 1996 SCH 8

The loss carry back rules contained in FA 1996 Sch 8 para 3 are aligned with the rules for trading losses and, accordingly, the carry-back period is reduced to a maximum of 12 months (previously, three years) preceding the accounting period in which the non-trade deficit was incurred. However, if that 12 months period has commenced prior to 31 March 1996, the loss carry-back is restricted to utilisation against loan relationship profits arising after that date.

AMENDMENTS TO FA 1996 SCH 11

Although life assurance is a trade, the legislation allows the Revenue to opt to tax a company's life assurance or capital redemption business not under Schedule D Case I but on the "I minus E" basis. That is, the income and gains of the life assurance or the capital redemption business (but not income gains from any other business carried on by the company) are assessed under the various Schedules and the Cases of Schedule D (other than Case I) and relief for expenses of management is given against this combined profit (which also includes the Case VI profits arising from reinsurance, pension and overseas life assurance businesses as well as the chargeable gains referable to basic life assurance and annuity business, "BLAGAB").

Almost invariably the Revenue will exercise their option to tax on the I minus E basis. Where a company carries on both life assurance and capital redemption business, separate I minus E computations are required.

The rules in FA 1996 Sch 11 para 4 relating to non-trade deficits apply where the I minus E basis applies and, again, the amendments to the loss carry-back rules are aligned to the rules for the carry back of trading losses; that is, 12 months are substituted for the previous three years relief. Because the rules require the non-trade deficit to be deducted from net income and gains before relief for expenses of management, it should be relatively rare for there to be an excess available to be carried back.

Since the rules for offsetting losses under I minus E are more complex than the general rules (as a result of ring fencing of certain income and gains, deferral of BLAGAB acquisition expenses and restrictions as to the maximum set-off of expenses of management against the BLAGAB income and capital gains) additional rules are required. The deficit carried back is required to be set-off against the loan relationship profits included in net income (referred to as "eligible profits") of the period, so long as it is all profit arising after 31 March 1996, but after deduction of expenses of management.

COMMENCEMENT AND TRANSITIONAL PROVISIONS—SUB-SS (7)–(12)

The amended FA 1996 Sch 8 para 3 and FA 1996 Sch 11 para 4 are to apply to non-trade deficits incurred in accounting periods ending on or after 2 July 1997.

However, where such an accounting period spans 2 July 1997, the losses incurred in that accounting period are to be split and the pre-commencement (ie pre-2 July 1997) part of the losses will continue to be eligible for a maximum carry back to a period beginning on 1 April 1996 (the balance of the losses only being eligible to be carried back for a maximum of 12 months). This rule is further amended by sub-s (9) for foreign exchange losses, where, for the pre-commencement losses which are carried back against foreign exchange gains, the maximum carry-back period remains a maximum of three years.

Generally, the losses will be apportioned on a time basis but, where time apportionment would work in a manner which would be unjust or unreasonable, the basis adopted can be some other method which will produce a just and reasonable result.

41   Restrictions on group relief

Schedule 7 to this Act (which imposes new restrictions on the giving of group relief) shall have effect.

GENERAL NOTE

This section introduces Sch 7, which provides a number of amendments to the rules for ascertaining the maximum amount of group relief (or consortium group relief) which may be claimed or surrendered by companies.

Capital allowances for small and medium-sized businesses

42   Temporary first-year allowances

(1) In subsection (1) of section 22 of the Capital Allowances Act 1990 (first-year allowances), after "40 per cent of that expenditure" there shall be inserted ", in the case of expenditure to which this section applies by virtue only of subsection (3C) below, shall be of an amount equal to the percentage of that expenditure that is given by subsection (1AA) below".

(2) After that subsection there shall be inserted the following subsection—

"(1AA) In the case of expenditure to which this section applies by virtue only of subsection (3C) below, the percentage mentioned in subsection (1) above is—

(*a*) in the case of expenditure to which Chapter IVA applies, 12 per cent; and

(*b*) in the case of any other expenditure, 50 per cent."

(3) After subsection (3B) of that section there shall be inserted the following subsection—

"(3C) This section applies to—

(*a*) any expenditure which, disregarding any effect of section 83(2) on the time at which it is to be treated as incurred, is incurred by a small company or a small business in the period beginning with 2nd July 1997 and ending with 1st July 1998; and

(*b*) any additional VAT liability incurred in respect of expenditure to which this section applies by virtue of paragraph (*a*) above."

(4) In subsection (4) of that section, after "any expenditure" there shall be inserted "to which this section applies otherwise than by virtue only of subsection (3C) above".

(5) After subsection (6A) of that section there shall be inserted the following subsections—

"(6B) No first-year allowance shall be made in respect of any expenditure to which this section applies by virtue only of subsection (3C) above—

(*a*) if the chargeable period related to the incurring of the expenditure is also the chargeable period related to the permanent discontinuance of the trade;

(*b*) if the expenditure (whether or not it is expenditure to which Chapter IVA would apply but for the provisions of section 38B) is expenditure of the kind described in any of subsections (2) to (4) of section 38B;

(*c*) if the expenditure is expenditure to which Chapter IVA would apply but for the provisions of section 38H;

(*d*) if the expenditure is expenditure on the provision of machinery or plant for leasing, whether in the course of a trade or otherwise;

and section 50(2) shall apply for the interpretation of paragraph (*d*) above as it applies for the interpretation of Chapter V of this Part.

(6C) No first-year allowance shall be made in respect of any expenditure incurred on the provision of machinery or plant to which this section applies by virtue only of subsection (3C) above if—

(*a*) the provision of the machinery or plant is connected with a change in the nature or conduct of a trade or business carried on by a person other than the person incurring the expenditure; and

(*b*) the obtaining of a first-year allowance is the main benefit, or one of the main benefits, which could reasonably be expected to arise from the making of the change."

(6) In sections 23(6), 42(9), 44(5), 46(8), 48(7) and 50(3) and (4A) of that Act

(which contain provisions referring to the temporary first-year allowances under section 22(3B) of that Act), after the words "subsection (3B)", in each place where they occur, there shall be inserted the words "or (3C)".

(7) In section 39(2)(*a*) of that Act (definition of a qualifying purpose), for "subsections (2) to (3B)" there shall be substituted "subsections (2) to (3C)".

(8) In section 43 of that Act (provisions relating to joint lessees in cases involving new expenditure), after subsection (4) there shall be added the following subsection—

> "(5) Any first-year allowance made in respect of expenditure to which section 22 applies by virtue only of subsection (3C) of that section shall be made on the same assumptions and subject to the same apportionments (if any) as it appears would, by virtue of subsection (3) above, be applicable in the case of a writing-down allowance."

(9) This section shall have effect in relation to every chargeable period ending on or after 2nd July 1997.

BACKGROUND NOTE

In consequence of the reform of capital allowances on plant and machinery in 1984, first year allowances ("FYAs") on plant and machinery no longer apply. Amendments to CAA 1990 s 22 were made to permit FYAs at the rate of 40 per cent on expenditure in the 12 months to 31 October 1993. Sections 42 and 43 amend, inter alia, CAA 1990 s 22 to provide FYAs at the rate of 50 per cent to small and medium-sized businesses on expenditure in the period 2 July 1997 to 1 July 1998 ("the relevant period").

GENERAL NOTE

Subsections (1) and (2) amend s 22 to provide that in relation to expenditure incurred by small companies or small businesses in the relevant period FYAs are available at the rate of 50 per cent (ie double the usual rate of 25 per cent writing down allowances) or, in the case of plant and machinery that constitute long life assets, 12 per cent (ie double the usual rate of 6 per cent writing down allowances).

ELIGIBLE EXPENDITURE

Subsection (3) inserts a new s 22(3C) which defines the expenditure to which the enhanced rates apply ie expenditure actually incurred in the relevant period (and not expenditure that by virtue of CAA 1990 s 83(2) would be treated as incurred in that period). It also provides that the enhanced rates apply to any additional amount treated as incurred (in respect of expenditure incurred in the relevant period) as a result of VAT being due under the Capital Goods Scheme.

Subsection (4) makes amendments consequential upon the introduction of sub-s (3).

LIMITATIONS AND ANTI-AVOIDANCE

Subsection (5) introduces a new s 22(6B) which—

> (*a*) prevents the granting of allowances at the enhanced rate if the expenditure is incurred in the period in which the trade is discontinued. In these circumstances relief should be given in the form of balancing allowances;
> (*b*) prevents allowances at the enhanced rate on certain vehicles, ships or railway assets (as defined in CAA 1990 s 38B(2)–(4), whether or not such assets would be "long life assets" as defined in s 38A);

(c) precludes allowances at the enhanced rate where the expenditure is on assets that, but for the transitional provisions of CAA 1990 s 38H, would have been treated as long life assets. This prevents expenditure incurred in the relevant period under a pre-26 November 1996 contract benefitting from 50 per cent FYAs given that under those transitional provisions it qualifies for 25 per cent, not 6 per cent, writing-down allowances;

(d) precludes allowances at the enhanced rate where the expenditure is on plant and machinery for "leasing" as interpreted by CAA 1990 s 50(2).

Subsection (5) introduces a new s 22(6C) preventing the enhanced allowances being available where the provision of machinery and plant is "connected" with a change in the way in which a trade or business is carried on (by a person other than that incurring the expenditure) where obtaining the enhanced allowances is (one of) the main benefit(s) expected to arise from the change. The Treasury's Notes on Clauses imply this subsection is aimed at large businesses, themselves not eligible for enhanced allowances, procuring third parties to incur expenditure on plant and machinery which, following the change in which the large businesses conduct their activities, could be used indirectly to benefit the large businesses.

CONSEQUENTIAL AND COMMENCEMENT

Subsection (7) makes a consequential amendment to CAA 1990 s 39(2)(a).

Subsection (8) applies the apportionment rules in CAA 1990 s 43(3) to expenditure qualifying for enhanced allowances.

Subsection (9) applies s 42 to chargeable periods ending after 1 July 1997.

43   Expenditure of a small company or small business

(1) After section 22 of the Capital Allowances Act 1990 there shall be inserted the following section—

"22A   Expenditure of a small company or small business.

(1) For the purposes of section 22 capital expenditure incurred by a company is capital expenditure incurred by a small company if the company—

(a) qualifies as small or medium-sized in relation to the financial year of the company in which the expenditure is incurred; and
(b) is not a member of a large group at the time when the expenditure is incurred.

(2) For the purposes of section 22, capital expenditure is capital expenditure incurred by a small business if—

(a) it is incurred by a business for the purposes of a trade (the "first trade") carried on by that business; and
(b) were the first trade carried on by a company (the "hypothetical company") in the circumstances set out in subsection (3) below, that company would qualify as small or medium-sized in relation to the financial year of that company in which the expenditure would be treated as incurred.

(3) Those circumstances are—

(*a*) that every trade, profession or vocation carried on by the business concerned is carried on by the business as a part of the first trade;

(*b*) that the financial years of the hypothetical company coincide with the chargeable periods of the business concerned; and

(*c*) that accounts of the hypothetical company for any relevant chargeable period were prepared in accordance with the requirements of the Companies Act 1985 as if that period were a financial year of the company.

(4) Subject to subsection (5) below, a company is a member of a large group at the time when any expenditure is incurred if—

(*a*) it is at that time the parent company of a group which does not qualify as small or medium-sized in relation to the financial year of the parent company in which that time falls; or

(*b*) it is at that time a subsidiary undertaking in relation to the parent company of such a group.

(5) If, at the time when any expenditure is incurred by any company any arrangements exist which are such that, had effect been given to them immediately before that time, the company or a successor of the company would, at that time, have been a member of a large group, this section shall have effect as if the company concerned was a member of a large group at that time.

(6) In this section—

"arrangements" means arrangements of any kind, whether in writing or not, including arrangements that are not legally enforceable;

"business" means—

(*a*) an individual;

(*b*) a partnership of which all the members are individuals;

(*c*) a registered friendly society within the meaning of Chapter II of Part XII of the principal Act; or

(*d*) a body corporate which is not a company but is within the charge to corporation tax;

"company" means—

(*a*) a company, or an oversea company, within the meaning of the Companies Act 1985; or

(*b*) a company, or a Part XXIII company, within the meaning of the Companies (Northern Ireland) Order 1986;

"financial year", "group", "parent company" and "subsidiary undertaking"—

(*a*) except in relation to a company formed and registered in Northern Ireland, have the same meanings as in Part VII of the Companies Act 1985; and

(*b*) in relation to a company so formed and registered, have the same meanings as in Part VIII of the Companies (Northern Ireland) Order 1986.

(7) References in this section, in relation to a company, to its qualifying as small or medium-sized—

(*a*) except in the case of a company formed and registered in Northern Ireland, are references to its so qualifying, or being treated as so qualifying, for the purposes of section 247 of the Companies Act 1985; and

(*b*) in the case of a company so formed and registered, are references to its so qualifying, or being treated as so qualifying, for the purposes of Article 255 of the Companies (Northern Ireland) Order 1986.

(8) In relation to a company with respect to which the question arises whether it is or would be a member of a large group, references to a group's qualifying as small or medium-sized—

(*a*) except in the case of a company formed and registered in Northern Ireland, are references to its so qualifying, or being treated as so qualifying, for the purposes of section 249 of the Companies Act 1985; and

(*b*) in the case of a company so formed and registered, are references to its so qualifying, or being treated as so qualifying, for the purposes of Article 257 of the Companies (Northern Ireland) Order 1986.

(9) For the purposes of this section a company is the successor of another if—

(*a*) it carries on a trade which, in whole or in part, the other company has ceased to carry on; and

(*b*) the circumstances are such that section 343 of the principal Act applies in relation to the two companies as the predecessor and the successor within the meaning of that section."

(2) This section shall have effect in relation to every chargeable period ending on or after 2nd July 1997.

GENERAL NOTE AND COMMENCEMENT

This section inserts a new CAA 1990 s 22A which contains definitions amplifying the provisions of s 42 and which applies to all post 1 July 1997 chargeable periods.

"SMALL COMPANY"

New s 22A(1) provides that expenditure is to be regarded as incurred by a small company if, by reference to CA 1985 (and its Northern Ireland equivalent) definitions, it is "small or medium sized" for the relevant financial year and it is not a "member of a large group" at the time the expenditure is incurred.

"SMALL BUSINESS"

New s 22A(2) provides that expenditure is to be regarded as incurred by a small business if it is incurred for the purpose of a trade carried on by that business and, if that business were carried on by a company, the company would be "small or medium sized" for the relevant financial year. Section 22A(3) provides assumptions for the hypothesis made by s 22A(2).

"MEMBER OF A LARGE GROUP"

New s 22A(4) is an anti-fragmentation section which provides that a company is a member of a large group if either it is the parent company of a group which is not small or medium sized or is a subsidiary undertaking in such a group.

Section 22A(5) provides that if there are arrangements in existence whereby a company or its successor could become a member of a large group but, if effect were given to those arrangements immediately prior to the relevant expenditure being incurred it would be a member of a large group, the company shall be treated as being such a member at the time the expenditure is incurred.

DEFINITIONS

Subsection (6) provides—

(*a*) a definition of "arrangements", relevant to sub-s (5);
(*b*) a definition of "business", relevant to sub-ss (2) and (3) including sole traders and partnerships composed solely of individuals;
(*c*) a definition of "company";
(*d*) for certain CA 1985 (or Northern Ireland equivalent) definitions to apply.

Subsections (7) and (8) provide the relevant company law definitions of small or medium-sized companies, namely satisfaction of two of the three following criteria for the current or preceding year—turnover not exceeding £11.2m, assets not exceeding £5.6m, not more than 250 employees—and membership of a larger group.

Subsection (9) imports the first part of the TA 1988 s 410(6) definition of "successor".

Capital allowances and finance leases

44 Writing-down allowances for finance lessors

(1) Section 25 of the Capital Allowances Act 1990 (qualifying expenditure for writing-down allowances) shall be amended as follows.

(2) After subsection (5) there shall be inserted the following subsections—

"(5A) Subject to subsection (5B) below, capital expenditure incurred by any person in any chargeable period on the provision of machinery or plant for leasing under a finance lease shall not be brought into account so as to form part of that person's qualifying expenditure for that period except to the extent of the part of the expenditure which is proportionate to the part of the chargeable period falling after the time when the expenditure was incurred.

(5B) Subsection (5A) above does not apply where, in the chargeable period related to the incurring of the expenditure, the disposal value of the machinery or plant falls to be brought into account in accordance with section 24(6).

(5C) Where under subsection (5A) above only part of any capital expenditure on the provision of any machinery or plant may be included in a person's qualifying expenditure for any chargeable period, subsection (1)(*a*)(*i*) above shall not prevent the whole or any part of the remainder of that expenditure from being included in his qualifying expenditure for the next following chargeable period."

(3) In subsection (6) (disposal values brought into account on an assignment)—

(*a*) for the words "subsection (5) above", in the first place where they occur, there shall be substituted "subsection (5) or (5B) above"; and
(*b*) for ", as modified by subsection (5) above," there shall be substituted "(as modified, where subsection (5) above applies, by that subsection)".

(4) In subsection (8) (adjustments), after "subsections (5)" there shall be inserted ", (5B)".

(5) This section has effect for chargeable periods ending on or after 2nd July 1997 except in relation to—

(*a*) expenditure incurred before that date; and
(*b*) expenditure incurred in the twelve months beginning with that date in pursuance of a contract entered into before that date.

GENERAL NOTE

This section amends the general provisions as regards entitlement to allowances where expenditure is incurred by finance lessors.

Subsection (2) introduces new sub-ss 25(5A)–(5C) into CAA 1990 which provide—

(*a*) that where expenditure is incurred on equipment to be leased under a finance lease only a proportionate part of the expenditure incurred in the chargeable period shall qualify for allowances in that period, ie the longer the period that has to run before the end of the period, the greater the proportion qualifying for allowances in that period;
(*b*) for new sub-s (5A) not to apply where the disposal value of the leased plant has to be brought into account under CAA 1990 s 24(6); and
(*c*) for the avoidance of doubt, that expenditure to the extent unallowed by virtue of sub-s (5A) in the first chargeable period may qualify for allowances in subsequent periods.

Effectively sub-s (5A) counteracts the benefit to finance lessors and, indirectly via reduced rentals, to lessees of lessors having several leasing subsidiaries with non-coterminous accounting periods where expenditure would be incurred by the relevant subsidiary shortly before the end of its accounting period and group relieved to other companies.

CONSEQUENTIAL AMENDMENTS AND COMMENCEMENT

Subsections (3) and (4) make consequential amendments to CAA 1990 s 25(6) and (8). Section 44 applies to chargeable periods ending after 1 July 1997 except in respect of pre 2 July 1997 expenditure and expenditure incurred prior to 2 July 1998 pursuant to a pre-2 July 1997 contract.

45   Hire-purchase by finance lessors

(1) In section 60 of the Capital Allowances Act 1990 (machinery and plant on hire-purchase), after subsection (2) there shall be inserted the following subsection—

"(2A) Subsections (1)(*b*) and (2)(*b*) above do not apply where the capital expenditure incurred by the person to whom the machinery or plant is treated as belonging under subsection (1)(*a*) was incurred on the provision of the machinery or plant for leasing under a finance lease."

(2) This section has effect for chargeable periods ending on or after 2nd July 1997 except in relation to—

(*a*) expenditure incurred before that date; and

(*b*) expenditure incurred in the twelve months beginning with that date in pursuance of a contract entered into before that date.

GENERAL NOTE

This section introduces a new CAA 1990 s 60(2A) disapplying s 60(1)(*b*) and (2)(*b*) where the expenditure by the person to whom the plant and machinery is treated as belonging by s 60(1)(*b*) was incurred to enable the equipment to be finance leased. The Treasury's Notes on Clauses indicate that, for finance lessors only, expenditure will be treated as eligible for allowances as it is incurred and not, as now, when the equipment is brought into use even though the expenditure may be incurred subsequently.

COMMENCEMENT

As with s 44, the new rules apply to post-1 July 1997 expenditure unless the expenditure was incurred prior to 2 July 1998 pursuant to a pre-2 July 1997 contract.

46   Sale and leaseback etc using finance leases

(1) In the Capital Allowances Act 1990—

(*a*) in section 75(1), (2) and (3) (further restrictions on allowances), for the words "sections 76 and 77", in each place where they occur, there shall be substituted "sections 76, 76A and 77"; and

(*b*) in section 76, after subsection (6) there shall be inserted the following subsection—

"(7) This section has effect subject to the modifications made by section 76A in cases where there is a finance lease."

(2) After section 76 of that Act there shall be inserted the following section—

"76A   Special provision for finance lease cases

(1) Where—

(*a*) any machinery or plant is used for the purposes of any non-trading activities carried on by any person, and

(*b*) it is directly or indirectly as a consequence of the machinery or plant having been leased under a finance lease that it is available for that use,

subsections (1), (2) and (3) of section 75 and subsection (1) of section 76 (except the words after "without") shall have effect as if the use for the purposes of those activities were a use for the purposes of a trade carried on by that person.

(2) Where—

(*a*) subsection (1), (2) or (3) of section 75 applies by virtue of paragraph (*b*) of that subsection, or is treated (under one or both of section 76(1) and subsection (1) above) as so applying,

(*b*) it is directly or indirectly as a consequence of the machinery or plant having been leased under a finance lease that it is available after—

(i) the date of the sale,

(ii) the date of the making of the contract, or

(iii) the date of the assignment,

for the use which is mentioned in that paragraph, or which is treated as if it were a use so mentioned, and

(*c*) apart from this subsection the disposal value to be brought into account under sections 24, 25 and 26 by reason of the sale, contract or assignment would be more than the amount ("the section 76(2) amount") which (if no disposal value fell to be brought into account) would be applicable instead in accordance with section 76(2) and subsection (5) below,

sections 24, 25 and 26 (and, accordingly, subsections (1) to (3) of section 75) shall have effect as if the disposal value to be so brought into account were equal to the section 76(2) amount.

(3) Where—

(*a*) a disposal value has fallen, in a case within sub-paragraphs (*a*) and (*b*) of subsection (2) above, to be brought into account under sections 24, 25 and 26 by reason of the sale, contract or assignment,

(*b*) the machinery or plant in question falls to be treated as belonging, at a time after the event by reason of which that disposal value fell to be brought into account, to any person in consequence of his incurring any capital expenditure,

(*c*) the allowances under this Part in respect of that capital expenditure are not restricted by subsection (1), (2) or (3) of section 75, and

(*d*) the amount of that expenditure ("the actual amount") exceeds the maximum allowable amount,

this Part shall have effect in relation to that expenditure as if it were expenditure of an amount equal to the maximum allowable amount.

(4) In subsection (3) above "the maximum allowable amount" means the sum of the following amounts—

(*a*) the disposal value falling to be brought into account as mentioned in subsection (3)(*a*) above, and

(*b*) so much of the actual amount of the expenditure as is equal to the amount included in that expenditure by virtue of section 66 (installation costs).

(5) In a case which—

(*a*) falls within paragraphs (*a*) and (*b*) of subsection (2) above, but

(*b*) is a case in which no disposal value falls to be brought into account as mentioned in the applicable subsection of section 75,

subsections (2) to (4) of section 76 shall have effect as if the amounts referred to in each of paragraphs (*b*) and (*c*) of section 76(2) were equal to the notional written-down value of the capital expenditure incurred by the person mentioned in that paragraph on the provision of the machinery or plant.

(6) Subsection (7) below applies where, in a case falling within paragraphs (*a*) and (*b*) of subsection (2) above—

(*a*) the finance lease, or

(*b*) any transaction or series of transactions of which it forms a part,

makes provision (otherwise than by means of guarantees from persons

69

connected with the lessee) the effect of which (if the lessor and the persons connected with him are treated as the same person) is to remove the whole, or the greater part, of any non-compliance risk which (apart from that provision) would fall directly or indirectly on the lessor.

(7) Where this subsection applies—

(*a*) subsections (1), (2) and (3) of section 75 shall have effect as if (as well as excluding the making of a first-year allowance), they also required—

(i) the whole amount of the expenditure, and
(ii) any additional VAT liability incurred in respect of it,

to be left out of account in determining the amount for any period of a person's qualifying expenditure under section 25; and

(*b*) subsections (2), (3) and (5) above shall not apply.

(8) Where subsection (7) above applies in a case where the buyer, person entering into the contract or assignee is different from the lessor—

(*a*) any capital expenditure incurred on the provision of the machinery or plant by the lessor, and
(*b*) any additional VAT liability incurred in respect of it,

shall also be disregarded both for the purposes of determining the amount for any period of the lessor's qualifying expenditure under section 25 and for the purposes of any claim by the lessor to a first-year allowance.

(9) In this section "the notional written-down value", in relation to any expenditure incurred by a person on the provision of any machinery or plant, means the amount which, if—

(*a*) the sale, contract or assignment were an event by reason of which a disposal value of that machinery or plant fell to be brought into account in that person's case, and
(*b*) the further assumptions set out in subsection (10) below were made in relation to that expenditure,

would give rise to neither a balancing allowance nor a balancing charge for the chargeable period for which that disposal value would be brought into account in that person's case.

(10) Those assumptions are—

(*a*) that the person in question incurred the expenditure on the provision of the machinery or plant wholly and exclusively for the purposes of a trade carried on by him (until its deemed discontinuance) separately from any other trade or other activities carried on or assumed to be carried on by him;
(*b*) that that person was within the charge to tax in respect of that separate trade;
(*c*) that the expenditure was the only capital expenditure ever taken into account in respect of that trade in determining qualifying expenditure for the purposes of section 24;
(*d*) that the expenditure is to be treated in relation to that person as expenditure to which Chapter IVA of this Part applies if, but only if, it is

expenditure falling in fact to be so treated apart from the preceding assumptions; and

(*e*) that there had been made to that person the full amount of every allowance to which, on the assumptions specified in paragraphs (*a*) to (*c*) above, that person was entitled in respect of that expenditure.

(11) This section and sections 75 and 76 shall have effect in relation to machinery or plant where—

(*a*) it is directly or indirectly as a consequence of the machinery or plant having been leased under a finance lease that it is available for any use to which it is put, and

(*b*) the machinery or plant has at any time been acquired by one public authority from another otherwise than by purchase,

as if the public authority from whom it was acquired were connected with the public authority that acquired it and with every person connected with the acquiring authority.

(12) In this section—

"deemed discontinuance", in relation to the trade assumed under subsection (10) above in a case in which section 75(1), (2) or (3) applies or is treated as applying, means a permanent discontinuance of that trade at the time of the sale, of the performance of the contract or, as the case may be, of the assignment;

"non-compliance risk", in relation to a finance lease, means a risk that a loss will be sustained by any person if payments under the lease are not made in accordance with its terms;

"non-trading activities" means any activities that do not constitute a trade; and

"public authority" includes the Crown or any government or local authority;

and (subject to subsection (11) above) references in this section to persons connected with each other shall be construed in accordance with section 839 of the principal Act."

(3) This section has effect for chargeable periods ending on or after 2nd July 1997 except in relation to expenditure incurred before 2nd July 1998 in a case in which—

(*a*) the sale referred to in subsection (1) of section 75 of that Act is a sale under a contract entered into before 2nd July 1997;

(*b*) the contract referred to in subsection (2) of that section is itself a contract entered into before 2nd July 1997; or

(*c*) the assignment referred to in subsection (3) of that section is an assignment made before 2nd July 1997 or in pursuance of a contract entered into before that date.

General note

This section restricts the capital allowances available to finance lessors where plant and machinery is sold to and leased back by a finance lessor to the original vendor. The Revenue are concerned to stop vendors who are unable to use allowances selling equipment to finance lessors at a price which enables the lessor to pass back to the lessee, in the form of reduced rentals, the benefit of the otherwise unusable allowances. The Revenue are also concerned about lease defeasance where, by various mechanisms, the risk of the lessee's default is reduced or eradicated. In these circumstances the finance lessor will not be entitled to any allowances.

Subsection (1) makes appropriate amendments to CAA 1990 s 75(1)–(3) and s 76 consequent upon the introduction into CAA 1990 of s 76A by s 46(2).

New s 76A provides—

(*a*) in sub-s (1) for s 75(1)–(3) and s 76 (which already restrict allowances where there is a sale and leaseback of equipment used for the purposes of an actual or deemed trade) to apply with the appropriate modifications where the equipment is used for non-trading activities in consequence of it being made available under a finance lease;

(*b*) in sub-s (2) for a restricted amount to be brought into account in the vendor's/lessee's computations under CAA 1990 ss 24–26, and hence the amount of expenditure qualifying for allowances in the lessor's computations. The restricted amount is based on that calculated in accordance with CAA 1990 s 76(2), broadly the lowest of open market value, cost to the seller or cost to a person connected with the seller, reduced further if appropriate by s 76A(5). Section s 76A(5) effectively substitutes a notional written-down value of the vendor or, if lower, that of a connected person for the cost to the vendor or to a connected person. The intention is to reduce allowances available to a lessor to the notional tax written-down value even if market value and/or purchase price of the equipment is higher;

(*c*) in sub-s (3) for the allowances to the lessor (if not already restricted by CAA 1990 s 75(1)–(3)) to be restricted to the "maximum allowable amount" if that is less than "the actual amount";

(*d*) in sub-s (4) a definition of "maximum allowable amount" being in effect the disposal value brought into the vendor's/lessee's computations in accordance with s 76A(2) with the addition of installation costs treated as additional expenditure on plant in accordance with CAA 1990 s 66;

(*e*) in sub-s (5) for the substitution of "notional written down value" (defined in s 76A(9)) for cost of the vendor or a connected person;

(*f*) in sub-s (9) that the notional written-down value of machinery or plant is such amount as would not give rise to a balancing charge or allowance if it were received on a disposal of the equipment based on the assumptions contained in sub-s (10) in the relevant chargeable period;

(*g*) in sub-s (10) that the assumed disponor is to be treated as having incurred expenditure only on the asset in question for the purposes of a notional separate trade within the charge to tax and has obtained all allowances that could have been made to him on the relevant asset. The asset is only to be assumed to be a long life asset if in fact it would be a long life asset; and

(*h*) in sub-s (11) that where assets have been acquired by a public authority otherwise than by purchase from another such authority (eg in a reorganisation or pursuant to a vesting order) all such authorities are to be treated as connected for these purposes where the asset is the subject of a finance lease.

DEFEASANCE ARRANGEMENTS

Section 76A(6) provides for sub-s (7) to apply (so as to prevent any allowances being available to the lessor, without any impact on the capital allowances position of the vendor/lessee) where a finance lease or "any transaction or series of transactions of which it forms part" have the effect of removing from the lessor and any person connected with him all or the greater part of "any non-compliance risk" to which the lessor (and/or connected persons) would be subject. "Non-compliance risk" is defined in sub-s (12). There is an exception where the non compliance risk is removed by guarantees from persons connected with the lessee.

Subsection (7) amends CAA 1990 s 75(1)–(3) in such circumstances to prevent any of the lessor's expenditure, including any expenditure treated as incurred as a result of the application of the Capital Goods Scheme causing VAT to be irrecoverable, from being eligible for writing-down allowances.

Subsection (8) extends the total block on allowances to a lessor where the asset was originally acquired pursuant to a contract or assignment of the benefit of a contract by a person different to the lessor.

DEFINITIONS

Subsection (12) defines—

(*a*) "deemed discontinuance", relevant to the sub-s (10) assumptions;
(*b*) "non-compliance risk", relevant to sub-s (6) and defeasance arrangements, as being the risk of loss if payments are not made in accordance with a lease's terms;
(*c*) " non-trading activities", relevant to sub-s (1); and
(*d*) "public authority", relevant to sub-s (11).

COMMENCEMENT

New s 76A applies to post-1 July 1997 transactions except where expenditure is incurred prior to 2 July 1998 where, as the case may be, the contract or the assignment was entered into prior to 2 July 1997 (or, in the case of an assignment executed after 1 July 1997, it was entered into pursuant to a pre-2 July 1997 contract to assign).

47   Meaning of "finance lease"

(1) After section 82 of the Capital Allowances Act 1990 there shall be inserted the following section—

"82A   Meaning of "finance lease"

(1) In this Part "finance lease" means any arrangements which—

(*a*) provide for machinery or plant to be leased or otherwise made available by a person ("the lessor") to another ("the lessee"); and
(*b*) are such that, in cases where the lessor and persons connected with the lessor are all UK companies—

(i) the arrangements, or
(ii) arrangements in which they are comprised,

fall, in accordance with normal accountancy practice, to be treated in the accounts of one or more of those companies as a finance lease or as a loan.

(2) In this section—

"accounts", in relation to a company, includes any consolidated group accounts relating to two or more companies of which that company is one;
"consolidated group accounts" means accounts prepared in accordance with—

(*a*) section 227 of the Companies Act 1985, or

(*b*) Article 235 of the Companies (Northern Ireland) Order 1986;
and

"UK company" means a company incorporated in a part of the United Kingdom;

and references in this section to persons connected with each other shall be construed in accordance with section 839 of the principal Act."

(2) This section has effect in relation to any case in relation to which the Capital Allowances Act 1990 has effect as amended by any of sections 44 to 46 above.

GENERAL NOTE

This section inserts, as a new CAA 1990 s 82A, a definition of a "finance lease" relevant to ss 44–46.

Films

48 Relief for expenditure on production and acquisition

(1) Subject to subsection (4) below, section 42 of the Finance (No 2) Act 1992 shall have effect in relation to any expenditure to which this section applies as if the following subsection were substituted for subsections (4) and (5) (which for any period limit relief for film production and acquisition expenditure to a third, or a proportionately reduced fraction, of the relievable expenditure)—

"(4) The amount deducted for a relevant period under subsection (1) above shall not exceed so much of the total expenditure incurred by the claimant on—

(*a*) the production of the film concerned, or
(*b*) the acquisition of the master negative or any master tape or master disc of it,

as has not already been deducted by virtue of section 68(3) to (6) of the 1990 Act, section 41 above or this section."

(2) Subject to subsection (3) below, this section applies to so much of any expenditure falling within paragraphs (*a*) and (*b*) of section 42(1) of the Finance (No 2) Act 1992 as is expenditure in relation to which each of the following conditions is satisfied, that is to say—

(*a*) the expenditure is expenditure incurred on or after 2nd July 1997 and before 2nd July 2000;
(*b*) the film concerned is a film with a total production expenditure of £15 million or less; and
(*c*) the film concerned is a film completed on or after 2nd July 1997.

(3) This section does not apply to so much of any expenditure falling within section 42(3) of the Finance (No 2) Act 1992 (acquisition expenditure) as exceeds the amount of the total production expenditure on the film concerned.

(4) Where this section applies to only part of any expenditure to which subsection (2) or (3) of section 42 of the Finance (No 2) Act 1992 applies in the case of any film, the amount deducted by virtue of subsection (1) of that

section for a relevant period shall not exceed the sum of the following amounts—

(*a*) the maximum amount of expenditure to which this section applies that is deductible for that period in accordance with subsection (1) above; and

(*b*) the maximum amount specified in subsection (5) below.

(5) The amount mentioned in subsection (4) above is the maximum amount which would be deductible for the relevant period in accordance with subsection (4) of section 42 of the Finance (No 2) Act 1992 if—

(*a*) in paragraphs (*a*) and (*b*) of that subsection (but not in paragraph (*c*)) the references to expenditure incurred by the claimant did not include references to any expenditure to which this section applies; and

(*b*) the maximum amount mentioned in subsection (4)(*a*) above had already been deducted by virtue of that section.

(6) In this section "total production expenditure", in relation to any claim for relief under section 42 of the Finance (No 2) Act 1992 in the case of any film, means (subject to subsection (7) below) the total of all expenditure on the production of the film, whenever incurred and whether or not incurred by the claimant.

(7) For the purposes of this section where—

(*a*) any part of the expenditure incurred by any person on the production of a film is incurred under or by virtue of any transaction directly or indirectly between that person and a person connected with him, and

(*b*) that part of that expenditure might have been expected to have been of a greater amount ("the arm's length amount") if the transaction had been between independent persons dealing at arm's length,

that part of that expenditure shall be deemed, for the purpose of determining the amount of the total production expenditure on the film, to have been expenditure of an amount equal to the arm's length amount.

(8) Subsection (3) of section 43 of the Finance (No 2) Act 1992 (time of completion of a film) shall apply for the purposes of this section as it applies for the purposes of sections 41 and 42 of that Act, but with the omission of paragraph (*b*) (completion on incurring acquisition expenditure) and the word "or" immediately preceding it.

(9) Subsections (3) to (6) of section 159 of the Capital Allowances Act 1990 (time when expenditure incurred) shall apply for determining when for the purposes of this section any expenditure is incurred as they apply for determining when for the purposes of that Act any capital expenditure is incurred, but as if, in subsection (6) of that section, the words "at a time" were substituted for the words "in a chargeable period".

(10) Section 839 of the Taxes Act 1988 (meaning of "connected person") applies for the purposes of this section.

(11) This section applies for the making of a deduction for any relevant period ending on or after 2nd July 1997.

BACKGROUND NOTE

Persons carrying on a trade or business involving the exploitation of films (in practice, producers or distributors) have, if the film concerned is a "qualifying British film", four options for the tax treatment of the cost of production or acquisition of the film. They may—

(*a*) write it off over the income-producing life of the film;
(*b*) write it off on a pound-for-pound basis as revenue is earned;
(both under CAA 1990 s 68(3)–(6);
(*c*) if the expenditure is capital expenditure and the income-producing life of the film is expected to last for at least two years, claim plant and machinery capital allowances (CAA 1990 s 68(9)); or
(*d*) write it off at a straight-line rate of 33.33 per cent per year from the time that the film is complete (under F(No 2)A 1992 s 42).

Options (*a*) and (*b*) are available in respect of any film (or tape or disc); options (*c*) and (*d*), on the other hand, are available only for a "qualifying film" (see below). Option (*d*) was introduced after representations from the film industry, since options (*a*) to (*c*) require the film to be producing income, whereas option (*d*) is available as soon as the film is complete. The time lag between completion and the generation of revenue can be considerable.

Following further representations that the 33.33 per cent rate of write-off was too slow, and a report from the Advisory Committee on Film Finance (chaired by Sir Peter Middleton), the new government has decided to allow an option for 100 per cent write-off on completion for all but the most expensive films. The 100 per cent write-off replaces the 33.33 per cent write-off, but only for a period of three years.

Q<small>UALIFYING FILM</small>

A qualifying film (a "British film") is a film certified as such by the Secretary of State under the Films Act 1985 Sch 1. Essentially, a qualifying film must be made in a Commonwealth or Irish studio by a maker who is either a person ordinarily resident in the EU or a company registered and managed in an EU member state. The bulk of labour costs must also be paid to Commonwealth or EU citizens or ordinary residents. There are additional requirements for minimum UK involvement.

E<small>XPENDITURE TO WHICH THE NEW RULES APPLY</small>

The new rules apply to expenditure incurred after 1 July 1997 and before 2 July 2000 on a film completed after 1 July 1997 the "total production expenditure" on which is no greater than £15 million (sub-s (2)).

The expenditure may be either production expenditure or expenditure on the acquisition of a qualifying film (sub-s (2); F(No 2)A 1992 s 42(1)(*a*), (2), (3)). Expenditure does not qualify if a deduction has already been claimed for it under CAA 1990 s 68(3)–(6) or a capital allowance made under CAA 1990 s 68(9).

The total production expenditure on the film is defined in sub-s (6) as the whole of the expenditure incurred on the production, whether by the claimant or any other person. This definition is subject to an anti-avoidance provision in sub-s (7) (see below).

A<small>MOUNT OF EXPENDITURE QUALIFYING FOR WRITE-OFF</small>

Subject to the constraints of sub-s (2), the amount of expenditure that may be written off under the new rules (F(No 2)A 1992 s 42(4), as substituted by sub-s (1)) is no more than the whole production or acquisition expenditure as has not already been deducted under CAA 1968 s 68(3)–(6) (see above) or written off as qualifying preliminary expenditure under F(No 2)A 1992 s 41 or previously under s 42.

LIMIT ON ACQUISITION EXPENDITURE

The amount of acquisition expenditure available for write-off under the new rules cannot be greater than the "total production expenditure" on the film (sub-s (3)).

EXPENDITURE PARTLY QUALIFYING: PREVENTION OF DOUBLE RELIEF

Subsections (4) and (5) together act to prevent double relief for expenditure that partly qualifies for the new rules and partly does not, and prescribe how relief is to be given in those instances.

In any period, the amount of the relief (the deduction permitted) cannot exceed the sum of—

(*a*) the amount qualifying under the new rules; and
(*b*) the amount that would qualify under the old rules assuming the maximum under the new rules had already been deducted.

EXAMPLE

Boötes Ltd, a film production company, incurs £9 million on a qualifying film "Voyage of the Argonauts", which is completed in its accounting period ended 31 December 2000. £4 million of this expenditure is incurred before 2 July 2000 and £5 million after that date.

The maximum deduction available for the y/e 31.12.2000 is—

Expenditure qualifying under the new rules:	£4,000,000
Maximum qualifying under the old rules:	
33.33% × (£9,000,000 − £4,000,000)	£1,666,667
	£5,666,667
Maximum deduction for the y/e 31.12.2001	
33.33% × (£9,000,000 − 4,000,000)	£1,666,667
Maximum deduction for the y/e 31.12.2002	
33.33% × (£9,000,000 − £4,000,000)	£1,666,667

WHEN A FILM IS COMPLETED

For the purposes of these rules, a film is completed when it is first in a form ready for distribution and presentation to the general public (sub-s (8), applying F(No 2)A 1992 s 43(3)(*a*)).

TIME WHEN EXPENDITURE IS INCURRED

Subsection (9) adopts the capital allowance rules of CAA 1990 s 159(3)–(6), with some modifications, for determining when expenditure is regarded as incurred for these rules.

ANTI-AVOIDANCE RULE

Subsection (7) contains a provision designed to counteract an artificial attempt to avoid breaching the £15 million barrier by underpaying a connected person.

Where any production expenditure is incurred as part of a transaction directly or indirectly between the person incurring the expenditure and a connected person, and the expenditure is less than the arm's length amount that would have been expected in a transaction between independent persons, the arm's length is substituted in computing the total production expenditure. No avoidance motive is necessary. A connected person is as defined in TA 1988 s 839 (sub-s (10)).

WHEN THE NEW RULES FIRST APPLY

The new rules first apply for accounting periods ending after 1 July 1997 (sub-s (11)).

PART IV

MISCELLANEOUS AND SUPPLEMENTAL

Stamp duty

49 Stamp duty on conveyance or transfer on sale

(1) Section 55 of the Finance Act 1963 and section 4 of the Finance Act (Northern Ireland) 1963 (both of which provide for rates of stamp duty on conveyance and transfer on sale) shall each be amended in accordance with the provisions of subsections (2) to (4) below.

(2) Subject to the modification mentioned in subsection (5) below, in subsection (1) (which specifies rates of stamp duty), for paragraphs (*b*) and (*c*) there shall be substituted—

"(*b*) where paragraph (*a*) above does not apply and—

(i) the amount or value of the consideration does not exceed £500, and
(ii) the instrument is certified as described in section 34(4) of the Finance Act 1958 at £250,000,

the rate of 50p for every £50 or part of £50 of the consideration;

(*c*) where paragraph (*a*) above does not apply and—

(i) the amount or value of the consideration exceeds £500 but does not exceed £250,000, and
(ii) the instrument is certified as described in section 34(4) of the Finance Act 1958 at £250,000,

the rate of £1 for every £100 or part of £100 of the consideration;

(*d*) where paragraphs (*a*) to (*c*) above do not apply and—

(i) the amount or value of the consideration does not exceed £500,000, and
(ii) the instrument is certified as described in section 34(4) of the Finance Act 1958 at £500,000,

the rate of £1.50p for every £100 or part of £100 of the consideration; and

(*e*) in any other case the rate of £2 for every £100 or part of £100 of the consideration;".

(3) In subsection (1A) (disregard of paragraph (*a*) to paragraph (*c*) of subsection (1) in relation to conveyances or transfers of stock or marketable securities) for "paragraph (*c*)" there shall be substituted "paragraph (*e*)".

(4) In subsection (2) (disregard of paragraph (*a*) for the purposes of leases where consideration includes rent which exceeds £600 a year)—

(*a*) after the words "shall have effect as if" there shall be inserted "(*a*)", and
(*b*) after the word "omitted" there shall be inserted—

"and
(*b*) in paragraph (*d*) for the words "paragraphs (*a*) to (*c*)" there were substituted the words "paragraphs (*b*) and (*c*)"."."

(5) In section 4 of the Finance Act (Northern Ireland) 1963, for the words "section 34(4) of the Finance Act 1958" wherever they occur, there shall be substituted the words "section 7(4) of the Finance Act (Northern Ireland) 1958".

(6) This section shall apply to instruments executed on or after 8th July 1997, except where the instrument in question is executed in pursuance of a contract made on or before 2nd July 1997.

(7) This section shall be deemed to have come into force on 8th July 1997.

BACKGROUND NOTE

Stamp duty is generally charged at the rate of 50p per £100 or part of £100 where there is a conveyance on sale of shares and securities: until the changes contained in s 49 were made, stamp duty ordinarily at the rate of £1 per £100 applied to transfers on sale of other dutiable property, subject to exceptions, specific provisions (eg in relation to leases) and transfers below the threshhold of £60,000.

GENERAL NOTE

Subsection (1) provides for amendments to be made both to FA 1963 s 55 and equivalent Northern Ireland legislation as regards transfers of all dutiable property (ie not just land and buildings) except stock and marketable securities.

Subsection (2) provides for a higher rate of duty of £1.50 per £100 or part thereof on transactions where the consideration exceeds £250,000 but does not exceed £500,000, and a higher rate of duty where the consideration exceeds £500,000 of £2 per £100 or part thereof. As with the previous regime the highest rate of duty applies unless the appropriate certificate of value is entered into, enabling the appropriate rate to apply to the whole of the consideration not just that in excess of the relevant threshhold(s).

Subsection (3) makes a consequential amendment as regards the provisions dealing with transfers of stock and marketable securities.

Subsection (4) makes similar amendments to the provisions dealing with calculation of duty paid under the heading "Lease or Tack" by reference to conveyance on sale duty on any premium paid on new leases where the average annual rent exceeds £600. In effect the same rates of duty apply to any premium, but duty in respect of the rental payments is unaffected.

Subsection (5) makes an amendment ensuring the appropriate cross reference as regards certificates of value for Northern Ireland transactions.

COMMENCEMENT

Subsection (6) provides that the higher rates apply to instruments executed after 7 July 1997 (see Stamp Act 1891 s 122 for the meaning of "execution") unless pursuant to contracts entered into on or before Budget Day.

As liability to duty is determined by the law in force at the time instruments are executed, sub-s (7) provides for s 49 to be deemed to have come into effect on 8 July 1997, irrespective of when F(No 2)A 1997 was enacted.

Provisional collection of taxes

50 Statutory effect of resolutions etc

(1) In section 1(3) of the Provisional Collection of Taxes Act 1968 (period for which resolution has statutory effect), after paragraph (*a*) there shall be inserted the following paragraph—

"(*aa*)   in the case of a resolution passed in February or March in any year, one expiring with 5th August in the same calendar year; and".

(2) In section 246(2)(*b*) of the Taxes Act 1988 (charge to ACT at previous year's rate until 5th May in any year), for "May" there shall be substituted "August".

(3) Subsection (1) above applies in relation to resolutions passed after the day on which this Act is passed.

Supplemental

51 Interpretation

In this Act "the Taxes Act 1988" means the Income and Corporation Taxes Act 1988.

52 Repeals

(1) The enactments mentioned in Schedule 8 to this Act (which include spent provisions) are hereby repealed to the extent specified in the third column of that Schedule.

(2) The repeals specified in that Schedule have effect subject to the commencement provisions and savings contained or referred to in the notes set out in that Schedule.

53 Short title

This Act may be cited as the Finance (No 2) Act 1997.

SCHEDULES

Section 1   # SCHEDULE 1

QUANTIFICATION OF A PRIVATISATION WINDFALL

The basic rule

1 (1) Subject to paragraph 7 below, where a company was benefitting on 2nd July 1997 from a windfall from the flotation of an undertaking whose privatisation involved the imposition of economic regulation, the amount of that windfall shall be taken for the purposes of this Part to be the excess (if any) of the amount specified in sub-paragraph (2)(*a*) below over the amount specified in sub-paragraph (2)(*b*) below.

(2) Those amounts are the following amounts (determined in accordance with paragraphs 2 to 6 below), that is to say—

(*a*) the value in profit-making terms of the disposal made on the occasion of the company's flotation; and
(*b*) the value which for privatisation purposes was put on that disposal.

GENERAL NOTE

The measure of the windfall in any case is the difference between the earn-out value of the company (the value in profit-making terms) and the value based on the price at which the company's shares were offered to the public on flotation (the value for privatisation purposes).

Value of a disposal in profit-making terms

2 (1) Subject to paragraph 4 below, the value in profit-making terms of the disposal made on the occasion of a company's flotation is the amount produced by multiplying the average annual profit for the company's initial period by the applicable price-to-earnings ratio.

(2) For the purposes of this paragraph the average annual profit for a company's initial period is the amount produced by the following formula—

$$A = 365 \times \frac{P}{D}$$

Where—

A is the average annual profit for the company's initial period;
P is the amount, ascertained in accordance with paragraph 5 below, of the total profits for the company's initial period; and
D is the number of days in the company's initial period.

(3) For the purposes of this paragraph the applicable price-to-earnings ratio is 9.

GENERAL NOTE

The earn-out value is ascertained by computing the average annual profits for the earn-out period (the "initial period") and multiplying by a P/E ratio of 9. Thus the value is $9 \times 365/D \times P$, where P is the "total profits" of the initial period and D is the number of days in that period.

Value put on a disposal for privatisation purposes

3 (1) Subject to paragraph 4 below, the value which for privatisation purposes was put on the disposal made on the occasion of a company's flotation is the amount produced by multiplying the institutional price by the number of shares comprised in the ordinary share capital of the company at the time of its flotation.

(2) In this paragraph "the institutional price", in relation to a company, means the highest fixed price per share at which publicly-owned shares in the company were offered for disposal on the occasion of the company's flotation.

(3) Subject to sub-paragraph (4) below, where publicly-owned shares in a company were offered for disposal in accordance with any arrangements for the payment of the price in two or more instalments, the price per share at which those shares were offered shall be ascertained by aggregating the instalments.

(4) Where the arrangements under which any publicly-owned shares in a company were offered for disposal provided for any discount on the payment of the whole or any part of the price for those shares, that discount shall be disregarded for the purposes of this paragraph in determining the price per share at which those shares were offered.

GENERAL NOTE

The value on flotation is the "institutional price" of the shares times the number of issued shares. The "institutional price" is the highest fixed price per share at which the shares were offered on flotation. This means the full price even if that price was payable by instalments and ignoring any discounts.

Cases where company privatised in stages

4 (1) For the purposes of this Schedule, where the disposal percentage in the case of any company was 85 per cent or less—

(*a*) the value in profit-making terms of the disposal made on the occasion of the company's flotation, and

(*b*) the value which for privatisation purposes was put on that disposal,

shall each be taken to be the disposal percentage of the amount which, under paragraph 2 or 3 above, would be the amount of that value but for this paragraph.

(2) For the purposes of this paragraph "the disposal percentage", in relation to any company, means the percentage which expresses (in terms of nominal value) how much of the ordinary share capital of the company at the time of

its flotation was represented by the publicly-owned shares in the company offered for disposal on the occasion of the company's flotation.

GENERAL NOTE

Where less than 85 per cent of the shares were offered for sale in the flotation, the earn-out value and the flotation value are each multiplied by the percentage offered on the flotation.

Total profits for the initial period

5 (1) For the purposes of paragraph 2 above the amount of the total profits for a company's initial period is the sum of the amounts falling within sub-paragraph (2) below.

(2) Subject to sub-paragraph (3) and paragraph 6(3) below, those amounts are every amount which, for a financial year of the company ending in or at the end of its initial period, is shown in the relevant accounts for that year—

(*a*) where those accounts are prepared in accordance with section 227 of the Companies Act 1985 (group accounts), as the profit of that company and its subsidiary undertakings for that year; and

(*b*) in any other case, as the profit of that company for that year.

(3) Where—

(*a*) any profit shown in the relevant accounts of a company for any financial year has been computed using a current cost accounting method, but

(*b*) the information which was contained in those accounts, or which was provided to the registrar together with those accounts, included information from which it can be ascertained what that profit would have been if an historical cost accounting method had been used,

the amount shown as that profit in those accounts shall be deemed to be the amount (as ascertained from that information) which would have been so shown if that historical cost accounting method had been used.

(4) In this paragraph references, in relation to any financial year of a company, to the relevant accounts are references to any such accounts for that year as have been or are delivered to the registrar under section 242 of the Companies Act 1985 and consist—

(*a*) in the case of a financial year at the end of which the company was a parent undertaking, in consolidated group accounts prepared in accordance with section 227 of that Act (group accounts); and

(*b*) in any other case, in accounts prepared in accordance with section 226 of that Act (individual accounts).

(5) Subject to sub-paragraph (6) below, references in this paragraph to the amount shown in any accounts as the profit for any financial year are references to the amount of the profit (if any) for that year which is set out in the profit and loss account comprised in those accounts as the item which is, or is the equivalent of, the final item of the statutory format which for that year was used for that profit and loss account.

(6) Where any amount shown in any accounts is less than it would have been if no provision or other deduction had been made—

(*a*) in relation to the windfall tax, or

(*b*) in anticipation of the imposition of a charge with characteristics similar to those of the windfall tax,

this Schedule shall have effect as if the amount shown were the amount it would have been if that provision or deduction had not been made.

(7) Nothing in this paragraph shall, in the case of any company—

(*a*) prevent any charge to windfall tax from being treated as having arisen on 2nd July 1997 by reference to accounts delivered to the registrar after that date; or

(*b*) prevent any requirement to pay an instalment of windfall tax, or any other liability under Schedule 2 to this Act, from arising before the delivery to the registrar of the accounts by reference to which the amount of that charge is computed;

and any power of the Board under that Schedule to make an assessment shall include power to make an assessment on the basis that accounts will be delivered to the registrar showing such amounts as may, to the best of their judgement, be determined by the Board.

(8) Subject to sub-paragraph (9) below, this paragraph shall have effect in relation to any time at which the Companies Act 1985 had effect without the amendments made by the Companies Act 1989—

(*a*) as if the references in sub-paragraphs (2) and (4) above to sections 226, 227 and 242 of the Companies Act 1985 were references, respectively, to sections 227, 229 and 241 of that Act, as it had effect without those amendments;

(*b*) as if the reference in sub-paragraph (2) above to a company's subsidiary undertakings were a reference to its subsidiaries (within the meaning of that Act as it so had effect); and

(*c*) as if the reference in sub-paragraph (4)(*a*) above to a company's being a parent undertaking were a reference to its having such subsidiaries.

(9) In relation to a company formed and registered in Northern Ireland, this paragraph shall have effect as if the references in sub-paragraphs (2) and (4) above to sections 226, 227 and 242 of the Companies Act 1985 were references, respectively, to Articles 234, 235 and 250 of the Companies (Northern Ireland) Order 1986.

(10) In this paragraph—

"the registrar" means—

(*a*) except in relation to a company formed and registered in Northern Ireland, the registrar within the meaning of the Companies Act 1985; and

(*b*) in relation to a company so formed and registered, the registrar within the meaning of the Companies (Northern Ireland) Order 1986;

and

"statutory format", in relation to a profit and loss account, means a format set out in the provisions (as they had effect in relation to that account) of

Schedule 4 to the Companies Act 1985 or Schedule 4 to the Companies (Northern Ireland) Order 1986.

GENERAL NOTE

"Total profits" for this purpose means the after-tax accounting profits, apportioned as necessary to the initial period where a financial year of the company straddles the start or end of the period. However, any provision for windfall tax is added back in arriving at such profits.

Meaning of the initial period etc

6 (1) In this Schedule "initial period", in relation to a company privatised by means of a flotation, means (subject to sub-paragraph (2) below) the period which—

(*a*) begins with the first day of the first financial year of the company to begin after the time of its flotation; and

(*b*) ends with the end of the fourth financial year of the company to begin after the time of its flotation.

(2) Where the initial period of a company privatised by means of a flotation would (but for this sub-paragraph) include any time on or after 1st April 1997, sub-paragraph (1) above shall not apply and the initial period of that company shall be taken, instead, to be the period which—

(*a*) begins with the day on which the time of its flotation falls; and

(*b*) ends with the end of the last financial year of the company to end before 1st April 1997.

(3) Where—

(*a*) sub-paragraph (2) above applies for determining a company's initial period, and

(*b*) there is a financial year of that company beginning before but ending after the beginning of that initial period,

the amount which for that year is shown as mentioned in paragraph 5(2) above shall be included in the sums added together for the purposes of paragraph 5(1) above to the extent only that that amount is attributable, on an apportionment made in accordance with the following provisions of this paragraph, to the part of that year falling within the company's initial period.

(4) Except in a case where sub-paragraph (5) below applies, an apportionment for the purposes of sub-paragraph (3) above shall be made on a time basis according to the respective lengths of—

(*a*) the part of the financial year falling before the beginning of the company's initial period; and

(*b*) the remainder of that financial year.

(5) Where the circumstances of a particular case are such that—

(*a*) the making of an apportionment on the basis mentioned in sub-paragraph (4) above would work in a manner that would be unjust or unreasonable, but (*b*) it would be just and reasonable to make the apportionment on the alternative basis,

the apportionment shall be made, instead, on the alternative basis.

(6) For the purposes of this paragraph an apportionment in the case of any company of the amount shown for any financial year as a profit for that year is made on the alternative basis where it is made according to how much of that profit accrued in each of the two parts of that financial year that are mentioned in sub-paragraph (4) above.

GENERAL NOTE

The initial period begins with the start of the first financial year of the company which begins after the date of flotation and ends with the end of the fourth financial year of the company which begins after that date. However, if the initial period as defined above would extend beyond 1 April 1997, then the initial period is the period beginning with the date of the flotation and ending with the end of the last financial year of the company to end before 1 April 1997.

Apportionment between demerged successors and predecessors

7   (1) This paragraph applies where—

(*a*) a company ("the predecessor company") was benefitting on 2nd July 1997 from a windfall from the flotation of an undertaking whose privatisation involved the imposition of economic regulation; and

(*b*) another company which on that date was a demerged successor of the predecessor company is also taken for the purposes of this Part to have been benefitting from such a windfall on that date.

(2) Where this paragraph applies—

(*a*) the amount of the windfall from which the predecessor company was benefitting on 2nd July 1997 shall be equal to only the appropriate fraction of the amount ("the total windfall") which (but for this paragraph) would have been the amount of that windfall under paragraphs 1 to 6 above; and

(*b*) the amount of the windfall from which the demerged successor shall be taken to have been benefitting on that date shall be equal to the remainder of the total windfall.

(3) In this paragraph "the appropriate fraction" means the following fraction—

$$\frac{P}{P+S}$$

Where—

P is the amount produced by multiplying the number of shares comprised at the end of the relevant day in the ordinary share capital of the predecessor company by the market price on that day of an ordinary share in that company; and

S is the amount produced by multiplying the number of shares comprised at the end of the relevant day in the ordinary share capital of the demerged successor by the market price on that day of an ordinary share in the demerged successor.

(4) For the purposes of this paragraph references to the market price of shares on any day are references to the sum of—

(*a*) the lower of the two prices shown in the Stock Exchange Daily Official List for that day as the closing prices for the shares on that day; and

(*b*) one half of the difference between those two prices.

(5) In this paragraph "the relevant day" means the day on which shares in the demerged successor were first listed on the Official List of the Stock Exchange.

G ENERAL NOTE

Where there has been a demerger of part of the undertaking at some time between flotation and 2 April 1997, so that both the original company (the predecessor) and the transferee company (the demerged successor) are within the charge to windfall tax, then the total windfall is apportioned between the companies by reference to the listed price value of the shares in the respective companies at the end of the day on which shares in the demerged successor were listed on the Stock Exchange Official List. The total windfall is the earn-out value of the two companies less the flotation value of the original company.

General interpretation of the Schedule

8 (1) In this Schedule "financial year", in relation to a company, means (subject to sub-paragraph (2) below)—

(*a*) a financial year of that company within the meaning of Part VII of the Companies Act 1985; or

(*b*) any period which—

(i) began before the coming into force of section 3 of the Companies Act 1989 (new definition of financial year); and

(ii) was a financial year of that company for the purposes of that Part, as it had effect without the amendments made by that section.

(2) Sub-paragraph (1) above does not apply to a company formed and registered in Northern Ireland; and in relation to such a company, references in this Schedule to a financial year are references to a financial year within the meaning of Part VIII of the Companies (Northern Ireland) Order 1986.

(3) In this Schedule references, in relation to a company privatised by means of a flotation, to the shares offered for disposal on the occasion of the company's flotation are references to the following shares in that company, that is to say—

(*a*) those that were the subject-matter of the offer to the public in respect of which that company is regarded for the purposes of this Part as having been so privatised; and

(*b*) any publicly-owned shares not falling within paragraph (*a*) above that were the subject-matter of an offer for disposal made on the same occasion as the offer mentioned in that paragraph.

(4) References in this Schedule to an offer for the disposal of shares in a company include references to any offer to transfer or confer an immediate or contingent right to or interest in any such shares, whether or not for a consideration; and (subject to sub-paragraph (5) below) references to the shares that are the subject-matter of such an offer shall be construed accordingly.

(5) For the purposes of sub-paragraph (3) above where—

(*a*) an offer for the disposal of publicly-owned shares in a company contained provision for a person to become entitled to further shares in that company if he satisfied conditions specified in the offer, and

(*b*) those conditions included a condition as to the period for which shares in that company continued to be held by that person,

shares which (apart from this sub-paragraph) would fall to be treated as the subject-matter of the offer by virtue only of that provision shall be treated as the subject-matter of the offer to the extent only that persons did in fact become entitled to them before 2nd July 1997 as a result of having satisfied the conditions in question.

(6) In this Schedule a reference, in relation to any time, to the ordinary share capital of a company is a reference to the following, taken together, that is to say—

(*a*) the shares comprised in the ordinary share capital of the company (within the meaning of the Tax Acts); and

(*b*) any shares that would have been so comprised at that time if the issued share capital of the company at that time had included any shares in the company that had been allotted but not issued.

GENERAL NOTE

This Schedule defines certain terms used in the computation of windfall tax.

Section 3 # SCHEDULE 2

ADMINISTRATION AND COLLECTION OF WINDFALL TAX

Returns

1 (1) The Board may by notice require any company which in their opinion is or may be a chargeable company to deliver to the Board a return complying with this paragraph.

(2) A company which has been required under this paragraph to deliver a return to the Board shall do so—

(*a*) except in a case where the Board's notice requiring the return is given after 1st November 1997, on or before 1st December 1997; and

(*b*) in the excepted case, before the end of the period of 30 days beginning with the day after that on which that notice is given.

(3) A return delivered to the Board under this paragraph must—

(*a*) set out the amount of windfall tax (if any) with which the company is charged;

(*b*) contain all such information about the matters mentioned in sub-paragraph (4) below as the Board may reasonably require; and

(*c*) be accompanied by all such accounts, statements and other records as the Board may reasonably require.

(4) Those matters are—

(*a*) the method used for the computation of any amount set out in the return as the amount of windfall tax with which the company is charged;

(*b*) the accounts, statements and other records by reference to which the computation of any amount so set out has been made;

(*c*) any group of companies of which that company is or has at any time been a member; and

(*d*) any other matters relevant to the extent of any liability of the company under this Part.

(5) A return delivered to the Board under this paragraph—

(*a*) shall be in such form as the Board may require; and

(*b*) shall contain a declaration by the person making the return that it is correct and complete.

(6) Where—

(*a*) a company has delivered a return to the Board under this paragraph, and

(*b*) that return sets out any amount as the amount of windfall tax with which the company is charged,

that amount shall be taken, except in so far as any other amount is assessed or otherwise determined under the following provisions of this Schedule, to be the amount of windfall tax with which that company is charged.

(7) Where—

(*a*) the Board have, at any time before the passing of this Act, given notice to any company requiring it to deliver a return, and

(*b*) that notice stated that it was given in anticipation of the passing of this Act and that, in the opinion of the Board, the company is likely to be a chargeable company,

that notice shall have effect on and after the day on which this Act is passed as if it were a notice given on that day in exercise of the power conferred by sub-paragraph (1) above.

GENERAL NOTE

The Board may issue a return to any company which it believes may be liable to the windfall tax. The return must be filed by 1 December 1997, or within 30 days after the date of issue, whichever is the later date. The contents of the return are specified.

Notification of liability and failure to make return

2 (1) If a chargeable company has not, before 1st December 1997, either—

(*a*) given notice to the Board that it is a chargeable company, or

(*b*) been required by a notice under paragraph 1(1) above to deliver a return to the Board,

that company shall be liable to a penalty of an amount not exceeding the amount of the windfall tax with which it is charged.

(2) A company which—

(*a*) has been required by a notice under sub-paragraph (1) of paragraph 1 above to deliver a return to the Board, and

(*b*) fails to deliver the required return in accordance with that paragraph,

shall be liable to the penalties set out in sub-paragraph (3) below.

(3) Those penalties are—

(*a*) a penalty of £3,000;

(*b*) in a case where the required return has not been delivered by the end of three months from the relevant time, a penalty (in addition to the penalty under paragraph (*a*) above) of an amount not exceeding 10 per cent of the amount of windfall tax with which that company is charged; and

(*c*) in a case where the required return has not been delivered by the end of six months from the relevant time, a penalty (in addition to the penalties under paragraphs (*a*) and (*b*) above) of an amount not exceeding 20 per cent of the amount of windfall tax with which that company is charged.

(4) In sub-paragraph (3) above "the relevant time", in relation to the delivery of a return, means the time by which that return should under paragraph 1(2) above have been delivered.

GENERAL NOTE

A company which is chargeable to windfall tax must give notice of liability to the Board by 1 December 1997 unless it has been sent a return by that date. There are penalties for failing to give notice of liability or failing to make a return on time.

Payment of windfall tax

3 (1) The amount of windfall tax with which a chargeable company is charged shall be paid by that company in two instalments as follows—

(*a*) one half of the amount charged shall be paid on or before 1st December 1997; and

(*b*) the rest shall be paid on or before 1st December 1998.

(2) The Board, if requested to do so, shall give a receipt for any windfall tax paid.

(3) The application by this Schedule of any enactment referring to the time at which an amount of tax becomes due and payable shall have effect, in relation to an amount of windfall tax, as if it referred to the time by which that amount is required to be paid under this paragraph.

GENERAL NOTE

The tax is payable in two equal instalments on 1 December 1997 and 1 December 1998 respectively.

General power to make assessments

4 (1) Subject to the following provisions of this Schedule, the amount of windfall tax with which a company is charged may be assessed on that company by the Board.

(2) An assessment of the amount of windfall tax with which a company is charged may be made whether or not any amount has been paid by that company in respect of that tax when the assessment is made.

(3) Subject to sub-paragraph (4) below, where—

(*a*) a company has delivered a return to the Board in pursuance of paragraph 1 above, and

(*b*) the Board are satisfied that the return is correct and complete,

the Board shall make an assessment in accordance with the return.

(4) The Board shall not be required to make an assessment under sub-paragraph (3) above in the case of a company whose return shows that it is not charged with windfall tax.

(5) Where the Board make an assessment under this paragraph in a case in which the assessment is not one which the Board are required to make under sub-paragraph (3) above in accordance with a return, the Board's assessment shall be made to the best of their judgement.

GENERAL NOTE

Assessments are made by the Board. An estimated assessment may be made in any case where the Board are not satisfied that the return is correct and complete; otherwise the Board must make the assessment in accordance with the return unless the return shows that the company is not liable for the tax.

Power to make assessments on discovery of unassessed liabilities

5 (1) If the Board discover that any company which—

(*a*) has made a return in relation to which paragraph 4(4) above applied, or

(*b*) has been assessed to an amount of windfall tax,

has not been assessed to as much windfall tax as it should have been, they may make an assessment or further assessment of the amount which, in their opinion, is windfall tax with which that company is charged but to which it has not been assessed.

(2) Where—

(*a*) the Board discover that an amount of windfall tax has been repaid which ought not to have been repaid, and

(*b*) that amount is not assessable under sub-paragraph (1) above,

that amount may be assessed by the Board, and recovered under this Schedule from the company to which it was repaid, as if it were an amount of windfall tax which that company is liable to pay.

(3) Where the amount of any assessment to windfall tax is reduced, the company assessed shall not for the purposes of this paragraph be treated, at any time after the reduction, as having been already assessed to the amount of windfall tax comprised in the reduction.

Supplemental provisions about assessments

6 (1) An assessment shall not be made under this Schedule at any time on or after 1st December 2003.

(2) Where an assessment is made under this Schedule, notice of that assessment shall be served on the company assessed.

(3) The notice of any assessment under this Schedule must state—

(*a*) the date on which it is issued; and

(*b*) the time within which any appeal against the assessment may be made.

(4) After the notice of any assessment under this Schedule has been served on the company assessed—

(*a*) the assessment shall not be withdrawn;

(*b*) the assessment shall not be amended, except in accordance with provision made or applied by this Schedule; and

(*c*) the company shall not, except in accordance with any provision so made or applied, be entitled to the repayment of any amount on the grounds that the amounts of windfall tax assessed on that company are excessive.

(5) Where notice of any assessment under this Schedule has been served on the company assessed, the amount of the assessment—

(*a*) shall be deemed (subject to the provisions of this Schedule) to be an amount of windfall tax with which that company is charged; and

(*b*) subject to the provisions of this Part about the payment of windfall tax in instalments, may be recovered accordingly.

(6) Liability to pay an instalment of windfall tax does not depend on the making of an assessment; and nothing in the provisions of this Schedule about

the making of assessments shall affect the times which are taken for the purposes of this Part to be the times by which companies are required under paragraph 3 above to pay instalments of windfall tax.

GENERAL NOTE

Notice of any assessment must be sent to the company assessed. No assessment may be issued after 31 December 2003. However, the payment of windfall tax does not depend on the making of an assessment.

Claims to relieve double assessment

7 (1) If, on a claim made to the Board, it appears to their satisfaction that a company has been assessed to the same amount of windfall tax more than once, the Board shall direct that so much of any assessment made on that company under this Schedule as appears to them to be excessive is to be vacated.

(2) A claim under sub-paragraph (1) above—

(*a*) must be made in such form as the Board may require; and
(*b*) shall not be made after the end of the period of six years beginning with the day of the service on the claimant of the notice of the most recent assessment to which the claim relates.

(3) On the giving of a direction under this paragraph with respect to any assessment, that assessment shall be vacated to the extent specified in the direction.

GENERAL NOTE

Where a company is assessed more than once in respect of the same amount of windfall tax, it may claim to have the assessment of any amount doubly assessed vacated.

Claims to correct errors or mistakes in returns etc

8 (1) If any company which has paid an amount of windfall tax assessed under this Schedule alleges that it has been, or continues to be, assessed to too much windfall tax by reason of—

(*a*) some error or mistake in a return under paragraph 1 above, or
(*b*) some error or mistake discovered by the claimant in a previous claim made by the claimant under paragraph 7 above or this paragraph,

the company may make a claim for relief under this paragraph in respect of that error or mistake.

(2) A claim under this paragraph—

(*a*) must be made in such form as the Board may require; and
(*b*) shall not be made—

(i) if it relates to an error or mistake in a return, at any time on or after 1st December 2003; or

(ii) if it relates to an error or mistake in a claim, at any time after the latest time at which that claim could have been made.

(3) On receiving a claim under this paragraph, the Board shall—

(*a*) inquire into the matter; and

(*b*) give, by way of repayment to the claimant, such relief (if any) as, having regard to all the relevant circumstances, they consider just and reasonable in respect of the error or mistake in question.

GENERAL NOTE

A company which has paid windfall tax on an assessment may claim error or mistake relief if it discovers an error or mistake in its windfall tax return or in a claim made under the preceding paragraph. Claims related to errors in returns must be made by 1 December 2003. Claims related to errors in claims must be made within the time limit for the claim itself.

Appeals against assessments and decisions on claims

9 (1) An appeal to the Special Commissioners shall lie against each of the following, that is to say—

(*a*) an assessment under this Schedule;

(*b*) a decision by the Board on a claim under paragraph 7 or 8 above.

(2) An appeal under sub-paragraph (1) above shall be made by notice to the Board.

(3) Subject to the following provisions of this paragraph, a notice of appeal under sub-paragraph (2) above—

(*a*) shall not be given more than 30 days after the day on which notice of the assessment or decision appealed against was given to the appellant; and

(*b*) must specify the grounds of appeal.

(4) An appeal under this paragraph may be brought out of time if, on an application made for the purpose by the appellant, the Board are satisfied—

(*a*) that the appellant has a reasonable excuse for not having brought the appeal within the time allowed by sub-paragraph (3) above; and

(*b*) that there was no unreasonable delay in the making of that application;

and, where the Board are not so satisfied, they shall refer the application to the Special Commissioners, who (if they are so satisfied) may themselves allow the appeal to be brought out of time.

(5) The Special Commissioners—

(*a*) may allow grounds in addition to those specified in the notice of appeal to be put forward on an appeal under this paragraph; and

(*b*) may take the additional grounds into consideration if they are satisfied that their omission from the notice was neither wilful nor unreasonable.

(6) Section 55 of the Management Act (postponement of tax to which an appeal relates) shall apply to an appeal under this paragraph against an assessment under this Schedule as it applies to an appeal against an assessment mentioned in subsection (1) of that section but as if, in that section—

(*a*) references to tax were references to windfall tax:

(*b*) references to the inspector were references to the Board; and

(*c*) subsections (6)(*a*) and (*b*)(*i*), (6A) and (9)(*a*) were omitted.

GENERAL NOTE

A company may appeal to the Special Commissioners against any notice of assessment to windfall tax or against any decision of the Board on a claim. Notice of appeal must be sent to the Board within 30 days of the date of the notice of assessment or decision. A late appeal may be accepted if there is a reasonable excuse for the delay.

Powers of Special Commissioners on an appeal

10 (1) Where there is an appeal to the Special Commissioners against an assessment under this Schedule—

(*a*) the Commissioners may, if it appears to them that the amount of the assessment is too much or too little, reduce or increase the amount of the assessment accordingly; and

(*b*) the assessment shall stand good if it is not reduced or increased under paragraph (*a*) above.

(2) Where an appeal is brought under paragraph 9 above against a decision of the Board on a claim under paragraph 7 or 8 above, the Special Commissioners shall hear and determine that appeal in accordance with the principles to be followed by the Board in determining claims under that paragraph.

(3) On an appeal to the Special Commissioners against a decision of the Board on a claim under paragraph 7 or 8 above, the powers of the Special Commissioners shall include power, if they think fit, to modify or cancel any decision made by the Board on that claim, including one made in favour of the appellant.

GENERAL NOTE

The Commissioners may increase or reduce any assessment appealed against and may determine any claim.

Procedures on appeal

11 (1) Subject to the following provisions of this paragraph, the following provisions of the Management Act shall apply for the purposes of and in relation to appeals to the Special Commissioners under paragraph 9 above as they apply for the purposes of or in relation to appeals to the Special Commissioners under the Tax Acts, that is to say—

(*a*) section 46A (regulations about the jurisdiction of the Special Commissioners);

(*b*) section 54 (settling appeals by agreement);

(*c*) section 56A (appeals from the Special Commissioners);

(*d*) sections 56B to 56D (regulations about practice and procedure etc).

(2) The Special Commissioners (Jurisdiction and Procedure) Regulations 1994

shall have effect, with the necessary modifications, in relation to appeals to the Special Commissioners under this Schedule as they have effect in relation to appeals to the Special Commissioners under the Tax Acts; but this sub-paragraph shall be without prejudice to the power of the Lord Chancellor, by virtue of sub-paragraph (1) above, to modify those regulations as applied by this sub-paragraph.

(3) Subject to paragraph 5 above and the provisions applied by sub-paragraphs (1) and (2) above, the determination of the Special Commissioners on an appeal under this Schedule shall be final and conclusive.

(4) Where an appeal has been made to the Special Commissioners against a decision of the Board on a claim under paragraph 8 above, neither the appellant nor the Board shall be entitled, by virtue of anything in sub-paragraph (1) above, to appeal except against so much (if any) of the decision of the Special Commissioners as relates to a point of law arising in connection with the computation in accordance with Schedule 1 to this Act of the amount of the windfall from which any company was benefitting on 2nd July 1997.

(5) Section 53 of the Management Act (appeal against the summary determination of a penalty) shall apply in relation to any summary determination of a penalty pursuant to—

  (*a*) the regulations applied by sub-paragraph (2) above, or
  (*b*) any modification of those regulations made by virtue of this Schedule,

as it applies in relation to any other such summary determination as is mentioned in that section.

(6) Subsections (2B) and (2C) of section 58 of the Management Act (Northern Ireland modifications) shall apply as if the reference to the Taxes Acts included a reference to this Schedule and, accordingly, as if the reference to section 56A of that Act included a reference to that section as applied by this paragraph.

(7) In the application for the purposes of this Schedule of—

  (*a*) section 58(2B) and (2C) of the Management Act, and
  (*b*) the regulations mentioned in sub-paragraph (2) above,

references to proceedings in Northern Ireland shall have effect as references to proceedings on an appeal to the Special Commissioners by a company whose head office or principal place of business is in Northern Ireland.

(8) Sections 21 and 22 of the Interpretation Act (Northern Ireland) 1954 (rules of court and powers of appellate courts) shall apply as if references in those sections to an enactment included a reference to sub-paragraphs (6) and (7) above.

GENERAL NOTE

Various provisions of TMA 1970 are applied for windfall tax purposes.

Interest

12 (1) Where any amount of windfall tax with which a company is charged is not paid before the time by which it is required to be paid under paragraph

3 above, that amount of that tax shall carry interest from that time until payment.

(2) Sub-paragraph (1) above applies to an amount whether or not the payment of that amount is postponed under section 55 of the Management Act (as applied by paragraph 9(6) above).

(3) Any amount paid by way of windfall tax which is repayable shall carry interest from whichever is the later of—

(*a*) the time by which that amount was required to be paid under paragraph 3 above, and

(*b*) the time when that amount was in fact paid,

until the time when that amount is repaid.

(4) The rate of interest under this paragraph for any period shall be—

(*a*) in the case of interest under sub-paragraph (1) above, the rate applicable under section 178 of the Finance Act 1989 for the purposes of section 87A of the Management Act (interest on unpaid corporation tax); and

(*b*) in the case of interest under sub-paragraph (3) above, the rate applicable under section 178 of the Finance Act 1989 for the purposes of section 826 of the Taxes Act 1988 (interest on overpaid corporation tax).

(5) Where any amount paid by way of windfall tax is repayable to a person who has paid interest under sub-paragraph (1) above, that person shall be entitled to a repayment of so much of that interest as would represent the interest paid on that amount if, after—

(*a*) making an appropriate apportionment of the payments made to the Board between the instalments due from the person making them, and

(*b*) taking account of any previous repayment,

it is assumed that the amount repayable is to be equated with the most recent payment or payments made to the Board.

(6) Interest under sub-paragraph (1) above—

(*a*) shall be paid without any deduction of income tax; and

(*b*) shall not be allowed as a deduction in computing income, profits or losses for any of the purposes of the Tax Acts;

and interest paid under sub-paragraph (3) above shall be disregarded in computing income, profits or losses for any such purposes.

General note

Interest on overdue windfall tax runs from the due date, whether or not the payment of any of it is postponed on appeal. If any tax is repayable, interest on the repayment runs from the later of the date of payment and the due date.

Collection of information

13 (1) For the purposes of this Part, section 20 of the Management Act (power to call for documents of taxpayer and others), together with sections 20B, 20BB and 20D(3) of that Act so far as they relate to section 20, shall be deemed to apply with the modifications set out in sub-paragraph (2) below.

(2) Those modifications are as follows—

(*a*) references to a tax liability shall be deemed to be references to a liability to pay an amount of windfall tax;

(*b*) references to an inspector shall be deemed to be references to any officer of the Board and references to the Taxes Acts shall be deemed to be references to this Part;

(*c*) in sections 20(7) and (8H) and 20B(1B) and (6)(*b*), the words "General or" shall be deemed to be omitted.

(3) For the purposes of this Part subsection (1) of section 98 of the Management Act (failure to comply with notice) shall apply as if this paragraph were included in the reference in column 1 of the Table in that section to Part III of that Act.

GENERAL NOTE

The Revenue's power to obtain information under TMA 1970 s 20 is extended to windfall tax, as are the penalty provisions of TMA 1970 s 98.

Penalties for furnishing false information

14   (1) Where a chargeable company fraudulently or negligently delivers an incorrect return in response to a requirement under paragraph 1 above, that company shall be liable to a penalty of an amount not exceeding the understated amount.

(2) In sub-paragraph (1) above "the understated amount", in relation to a return delivered by a chargeable company, means the amount (if any) by which the amount of windfall tax with which that company is charged exceeds the amount set out in the return as the amount with which it is charged.

(3) For the purposes of this Part—

(*a*) subsection (2) of section 98 of the Management Act (penalties for furnishing incorrect information etc) shall apply as if the provisions of this Schedule (except paragraph 1) were specified in one of the columns of the Table in that section; and

(*b*) section 99 of that Act (penalty for assisting in preparation of incorrect return) shall apply as if the reference in paragraph (*a*) of that section to tax included a reference to windfall tax.

(4) Section 97(1) of the Management Act (obligation to correct incorrect return) shall apply for the purposes of this paragraph in relation to a return delivered in response to a requirement under paragraph 1 above as it applies for the purposes of section 96 of that Act in relation to such a return as is mentioned in that section.

GENERAL NOTE

Various enforcement provisions of TMA 1970 are applied for windfall tax purposes.

Recovery of tax

15 (1) The provisions of the Management Act which are set out in sub-paragraph (2) below (which all relate to the recovery of tax) shall apply, subject to the modifications set out in sub-paragraph (3) below, in relation to—

(*a*) amounts of windfall tax due from any company,

(*b*) any penalty under this Schedule, or

(*c*) any interest for which a company is liable under paragraph 12 above or 17(5)(*g*) below,

as they apply in relation to sums charged by way of tax; and, in the case of amounts falling within paragraph (*b*) or (*c*) above, those provisions shall so apply as if those amounts were amounts of tax due and payable under an assessment.

(2) The provisions applied by sub-paragraph (1) above are—

(*a*) section 61 (distraint);

(*b*) sections 63 and 63A (recovery in Scotland);

(*c*) sections 66 to 68 (court proceedings for the recovery of tax);

(*d*) section 70(1) (certificate of non-payment); and

(*e*) section 70A (payment by cheque).

(3) The modifications mentioned in that sub-paragraph are as follows—

(*a*) in all those provisions references to the collector shall be deemed to include references to any other officer of the Board;

(*b*) in section 63, the words "under section 60 of this Act" in subsection (1)(*b*) shall be deemed to be omitted and so shall subsections (3) and (4); and

(*c*) in section 70A—

(i) the reference in subsection (1) to the purposes of the Management Act and the provisions mentioned in subsection (2) of that section shall be deemed to be a reference to the purposes of this Part; and

(ii) subsection (2) shall be deemed to be omitted.

Recovery against other group members

16 (1) Subject to sub-paragraph (3) below, where any amount of windfall tax with which a company is charged is not paid before the end of the period of six months beginning with the time by which it was required to be paid under paragraph 3 above ("the six month period"), any company falling within sub-paragraph (2) below may be assessed (in the name of the chargeable company) to all or any part of the unpaid windfall tax with which the chargeable company is charged.

(2) A company falls within this sub-paragraph if it is one or other or both of the following, that is to say—

(*a*) a member of the same group as the chargeable company at the end of the six month period; or

(*b*) a company which has been a member of the same group as the chargeable company at some time on or after 2nd July 1997 and before the end of the six month period.

(3) A company shall not be assessed under sub-paragraph (1) above to any amount of windfall tax at any time more than two years after that company first became assessable to that amount under that sub-paragraph.

(4) This Schedule shall have effect for the purposes of, and in relation to, an assessment under sub-paragraph (1) above as if the amount to which a company is assessable under this paragraph were an amount of windfall tax with which that company is charged.

(5) Where, by virtue of this paragraph, any company ("the group member") pays any amount of windfall tax with which another company ("the charged company") is charged—

(*a*) that payment shall discharge the liability of the charged company to pay that amount of windfall tax; but

(*b*) the group member shall be entitled to recover from the charged company the whole amount paid, together with any interest paid by the group member on that amount by virtue of paragraph 12 above.

GENERAL NOTE

Any windfall tax not paid within six months of the due date may be recovered from members of the same group as the chargeable company.

General provisions about penalties etc

17 (1) Where a company which has become liable to a tax-geared penalty subsequently becomes liable to another such penalty, the amount or, as the case may be, maximum amount of the subsequent penalty shall be treated as reduced so that the aggregate of the tax-geared penalties to which the company has become liable does not exceed the greater or greatest of them.

(2) In sub-paragraph (1) above "tax-geared penalty" means (subject to sub-paragraph (3) below)—

(*a*) a penalty under paragraph 2(1) or 14(1) above; or

(*b*) a penalty under paragraph 2(2) above falling within paragraph 2(3)(*b*) or (*c*) above.

(3) Where a company has become liable to both—

(*a*) a penalty falling within paragraph 2(3)(*b*) above; and

(*b*) a penalty falling within paragraph 2(3)(*c*) above,

the aggregate of those penalties shall be treated as only one tax-geared penalty for the purposes of sub-paragraph (1) above.

(4) The provisions of the Management Act set out in sub-paragraph (5) below shall apply, subject to the modifications set out in sub-paragraph (6) below, in relation to penalties under this Schedule as they apply in relation to the penalties mentioned in those provisions.

(5) The provisions applied by sub-paragraph (4) above are—

(*a*) section 100 (determination of penalties);

(*b*) section 100A(2) and (3) (provision supplementary to section 100);

(*c*) section 100C (penalty proceedings before Commissioners);

(*d*) section 100D (penalty proceedings before courts);

(*e*) section 102 (mitigation of penalties);

(*f*) section 103 (time limit for penalty proceedings); and

(*g*) section 103A (interest on penalties).

(6) The modifications mentioned in that sub-paragraph are—

(*a*) in section 100(2), for the words from "a penalty" onwards there shall be deemed to be substituted a reference to a penalty by virtue of paragraph 13(3) above;

(*b*) subsection (6) of section 100 shall be deemed to be omitted;

(*c*) in section 100A(3), the reference to tax shall be deemed to be a reference to windfall tax;

(*d*) in section 100C(1), the words "General or" shall be deemed to be omitted; and

(*e*) in section 103, the references to tax in subsection (1) shall be deemed to be references to windfall tax, and subsection (2) shall be deemed to be omitted.

(7) An appeal may be brought against any determination under section 100 of the Management Act of a penalty under this Schedule.

(8) Subject to sub-paragraph (9) below, the provisions of this Schedule relating to an appeal against an assessment to windfall tax shall apply (with the necessary modifications) in relation to any appeal under sub-paragraph (7) above.

(9) Paragraph 10 above shall not apply to an appeal under sub-paragraph (7) above and the powers of the Special Commissioners on an appeal under that sub-paragraph shall be those set out in section 100B(2)(*a*) and (*b*) of the Management Act.

(10) Subsection (3) of section 100B of the Management Act (further appeals) shall apply where there has been an appeal under sub-paragraph (7) above as it applies where there has been an appeal under subsection (1) of that section.

(11) The liabilities of any person under this Part shall be without prejudice to any criminal liability arising in relation to the same matter.

GENERAL NOTE

The penalty provisions of TMA 1970 ss 100–103A are applied for windfall tax purposes.

Miscellaneous applications

18 (1) The provisions of the Management Act which are set out in sub-paragraph (2) below shall apply for the purposes of this Schedule—

(*a*) as they apply for the purposes of the enactments for the purposes of which they have effect apart from this paragraph; but

(*b*) as if any reference in those provisions to a tax included a reference to windfall tax.

(2) Those provisions are—

(*a*) section 75 (receivers);

(*b*) section 105 (evidence in cases of fraudulent conduct);

(*c*) section 108 (company officers);

(*d*) section 112 (lost documents etc);

(*e*) section 113(3) (prescription of form of assessments, penalty determinations);

(*f*) section 114 (provision for errors not to invalidate an assessment);

(*g*) section 115 (delivery and service of documents) and the regulations made under that section; and

(*h*) section 118(2) and (4) (extensions of time, reasonable excuse for delay and finality of assessments).

GENERAL NOTE

Various other provisions of TMA 1970 are applied for windfall tax purposes.

Interpretation

19   (1) In this Schedule—

"the Board" means the Commissioners of Inland Revenue;

"chargeable company" means a company which, on 2nd July 1997, was benefitting from a windfall from the flotation of an undertaking whose privatisation involved the imposition of economic regulation;

"group" means a parent undertaking (within the meaning of the Companies Act 1985 or the Companies (Northern Ireland) Order 1986), together with all of its subsidiary undertakings;

"the Management Act" means the Taxes Management Act 1970;

"notice" means notice in writing;

"Special Commissioners" has the same meaning as in the Tax Acts.

(2) In this Schedule references to the repayment of an amount of windfall tax include references to making an allowance by way of set-off of an amount of windfall tax against any liability.

(3) References in this Schedule to a penalty under this Schedule include references to a penalty under a provision of the Management Act as applied by this Schedule.

GENERAL NOTE

Various other terms are defined.

SCHEDULE 3

INSURANCE COMPANIES AND FRIENDLY SOCIETIES

GENERAL NOTE

Section 19 to this Act removes the entitlement of pension funds to recover tax credits in respect of dividends of UK companies made on or after 2 July 1997. Schedule 3 reflects these changes in relation to an insurance company's entitlement to payment of tax credits relating to its pension business in respect of dividends and other company distributions made on or after 2 July 1997. Changes are also introduced to the rules that determine how much of a life insurance company's profits are charged to different rates of corporation tax following upon the withdrawal of a company's entitlement to have pension business tax credits paid to it.

Other changes not noted below are made to simplify the existing rules about including dividends and other company distributions when calculating the profit or loss an insurance company makes from its total life assurance business which is considered separately for tax purposes, such as pension business, life re-insurance and overseas life assurance business.

Section 76 of the Taxes Act 1988

1 (1) Section 76 of the Taxes Act 1988 (expenses of management: insurance companies) shall be amended as follows.

(2) In subsection (2B) (relevant income from life assurance business to be sum of items in paragraphs (*a*) and (*b*)) for paragraph (*b*) (relevant franked investment income) there shall be substituted—

"(*b*) the franked investment income of, and foreign income dividends arising to, the company which are referable to its basic life assurance and general annuity business."

(3) In subsection (8) (interpretation) the definition of "relevant franked investment income" shall cease to have effect.

(4) This paragraph has effect in relation to distributions made on or after 2nd July 1997.

Section 432E of the Taxes Act 1988

2 (1) In section 432E of the Taxes Act 1988 (section 432B apportionment: participating funds) paragraph (*b*) of subsection (6) (which provides for the adjustment of the net amount referable to overseas life assurance business) shall cease to have effect.

(2) This paragraph has effect in relation to distributions made on or after 2nd July 1997.

Section 434 of the Taxes Act 1988

3 (1) Section 434 of the Taxes Act 1988 (franked investment income etc) shall be amended as follows.

(2) For subsection (1) (nothing in section 208 prevents franked investment

income or foreign income dividends from being taken into account in computations made for the purposes of section 89(7) of the Finance Act 1989 or section 76(2)) there shall be substituted—

"(1) Section 208 shall not apply in relation to—

(*a*) the charge to corporation tax on the life assurance profits of an insurance company computed in accordance with the provisions of this Act applicable to Case I of Schedule D; or

(*b*) any computation of such profits in accordance with those provisions.

(1A) Paragraph 2 of Schedule F shall not have effect for the purposes of subsection (1)(*a*) or (*b*) above, but this subsection shall not apply in relation to distributions in respect of which an insurance company is entitled to a tax credit under section 441A.

(1B) The reference in subsection (1) above to the life assurance profits of an insurance company is a reference to the profits of the company—

(*a*) in respect of its life assurance business; or

(*b*) in respect of any category of life assurance business which it carries on."

(3) In subsection (3) (certain franked investment income not to be used to frank distributions but may be the subject of claim under section 242) the words from "but it may be the subject of a claim" onwards shall cease to have effect.

(4) In subsection (8) (which provides amongst other things for the payment of tax credit) the words from "or by payment of tax credit" onwards shall cease to have effect.

(5) Sub-paragraph (2) above has effect in relation to distributions made on or after 2nd July 1997.

(6) Sub-paragraph (3) above has effect for accounting periods beginning on or after 2nd July 1997.

(7) Sub-paragraph (4) above has effect for accounting periods beginning on or after 1st January 1998.

(8) In determining, for the purposes of any claim under section 242 of the Taxes Act 1988 made by virtue of section 434(3) of that Act for an accounting period beginning before 2nd July 1997 and ending on or after that date, the policy holders' share of the franked investment income from investments held in connection with an insurance company's life assurance business, there shall be left out of account any distributions which are made on or after 2nd July 1997.

(9) Any amount which, by virtue of sub-paragraph (8) above, is treated as a surplus of franked investment income for the purposes of any such claim as is mentioned in that sub-paragraph shall be disregarded for the purposes of section 20(4) of this Act.

Section 434A of the Taxes Act 1988

4 (1) In section 434A of the Taxes Act 1988 (computation of losses and limitation on relief) subsection (1) (which falls as a result of new section 434(1) to (1B)) shall cease to have effect.

(2) This paragraph has effect for accounting periods beginning on or after 2nd July 1997.

Section 436 of the Taxes Act 1988

5 (1) In section 436 of the Taxes Act 1988 (pension business: separate charge on profits) in subsection (3), paragraphs (*d*) and (*e*) (which make provision, for the purposes of the computation of profits arising from pension business, for group income and non-qualifying distributions to be left out of account) shall cease to have effect.

(2) This paragraph has effect in relation to distributions made on or after 2nd July 1997.

Section 438 of the Taxes Act 1988

6 (1) Section 438 of the Taxes Act 1988 (pension business: exemption from tax) shall be amended as follows.

(2) Subsections (3) and (3AA) (which fall as a result of section 434(1) to (1B)) shall cease to have effect.

(3) For subsection (4) (which makes provision in relation to the payment of tax credits) there shall be substituted—

"(4) This section shall be disregarded in determining, in relation to an insurance company which is entitled to a tax credit in respect of a distribution, whether the condition in paragraph (*a*) or (*b*) of section 231(2) is satisfied."

(4) Subsection (5) (which falls with the substitution of subsection (4)) shall cease to have effect.

(5) Subsections (6) to (7) (which fall with the repeal of subsections (3), (3AA) and (5) and the substitution of subsection (4)) shall cease to have effect.

(6) Subsection (9) (which falls with the repeal of subsections (6), (6B) and (6E) and the repeal of section 440B(2)) shall cease to have effect.

(7) Sub-paragraphs (2) to (4) above have effect in relation to distributions made on or after 2nd July 1997.

(8) Sub-paragraphs (5) and (6) above have effect for accounting periods beginning on or after 2nd July 1997.

(9) In determining, for the purposes of subsections (6) to (7) of section 438 of the Taxes Act 1988, the franked investment income of, or foreign income dividends arising to, an insurance company for an accounting period beginning before 2nd July 1997 and ending on or after that date, there shall be left out of account any distributions which are made on or after 2nd July 1997.

GENERAL NOTE

Subparagraph (3) is the substantive provision removing from 2 July 1997 the entitlement to payment of tax credits in respect of dividends and other distributions attributable to insured pension business. The result of this change is to treat insured pensions in the same way as uninsured pensions are to be treated as a result of s 19 of this Act.

Section 439B of the Taxes Act 1988

7 (1) In section 439B of the Taxes Act 1988 (life reinsurance business: separate charge on profits) subsection (7) (which falls as a result of section 434(1) to (1B)) shall cease to have effect.

(2) This paragraph has effect in relation to distributions made on or after 2nd July 1997.

Section 440B of the Taxes Act 1988

8 (1) Section 440B of the Taxes Act 1988 (modifications where tax charged under Case I of Schedule D) shall be amended as follows.

(2) Subsection (1A) (which falls as a result of new section 434(1) to (1B)) shall cease to have effect.

(3) Subsection (2) (which falls with the repeal of section 438(6), (6B) and (6E)) shall cease to have effect.

(4) Sub-paragraph (2) above has effect in relation to distributions made on or after 2nd July 1997.

(5) Sub-paragraph (3) above has effect for accounting periods beginning on or after 2nd July 1997.

Section 441A of the Taxes Act 1988

9 (1) Section 441A of the Taxes Act 1988 (section 441: distributions) shall be amended as follows.

(2) Subsection (1) (which falls as a result of new section 434(1) to (1B)) shall cease to have effect.

(3) In subsection (2), for "such a distribution" there shall be substituted "a distribution in respect of any asset of its overseas life assurance fund".

(4) This paragraph has effect in relation to distributions made on or after 2nd July 1997.

Schedule 19AB to the Taxes Act 1988

10 (1) Schedule 19AB to the Taxes Act 1988 (payments on account of tax credits and deducted tax) shall be amended as follows.

(2) In paragraph 1 (entitlement to certain payments on account) in sub-paragraph (1)—

(*a*) the words "the aggregate of" shall cease to have effect; and
(*b*) paragraph (*b*) (which confers entitlement to payments in respect of tax credits) shall cease to have effect.

(3) In sub-paragraph (7) of that paragraph, as that sub-paragraph has effect apart from the provisions of paragraph 1(6) of Schedule 34 to the Finance Act 1996—

(*a*) the words "paid or" shall cease to have effect;
(*b*) paragraph (*b*) shall cease to have effect; and
(*c*) in the words following paragraph (*b*), the words "or in section 42(5A) of the Management Act" shall cease to have effect.

(4) Sub-paragraph (8) (which falls with the repeal of section 438(6)) shall cease to have effect.

(5) In sub-paragraph (10) (which defines "pension business repayments")—

　(*a*) the words "and payments of tax credits", and
　(*b*) the words "or in section 42(5A) of the Management Act",

shall cease to have effect.

(6) Sub-paragraph (2) above has effect in relation to distributions made on or after 2nd July 1997.

(7) Sub-paragraphs (3) to (5) above have effect for accounting periods beginning on or after 2nd July 1997.

11 (1) Schedule 19AB to the Taxes Act 1988, as it has effect in relation to provisional repayment periods falling in accounting periods ending on or after the day appointed under section 199 of the Finance Act 1994 for the purposes of Chapter III of Part IV of that Act, shall be amended as follows.

(2) In paragraph 1, in sub-paragraph (7)—

　(*a*) the words "paid or" shall cease to have effect;
　(*b*) paragraph (*b*) shall cease to have effect; and
　(*c*) in the words following paragraph (*b*), the words "or section 42(4) of the Management Act" shall cease to have effect.

(3) In paragraph 3 (repayment with interest of excessive provisional repayments) in sub-paragraph (1A)—

　(*a*) the words "paid or" shall cease to have effect;
　(*b*) the words "or section 42(4) of the Management Act" shall cease to have effect; and
　(*c*) paragraph (*b*) shall cease to have effect.

(4) In sub-paragraph (1B) of that paragraph—

　(*a*) the words "payments or" shall cease to have effect; and
　(*b*) paragraph (*b*) shall cease to have effect.

(5) In sub-paragraph (8) of that paragraph—

　(*a*) the words "paid or" shall cease to have effect; and
　(*b*) paragraph (*b*) shall cease to have effect.

GENERAL NOTE

Paragraphs 10 and 11 ensure that, as a result of the abolition of payment of pension business tax credits, a company cannot make a claim to in-year payments on account of tax credits under the special rules applicable to insurance companies.

12 (1) For the purposes of section 121 of the Finance Act 1993 (repayments and payments to friendly societies), Schedule 19AB to the Taxes Act 1988 shall be deemed to have effect without the amendments made by this Schedule.

(2) In relation to distributions made on or after 6th April 1999, sub-paragraph (1) above shall not prevent Schedule 19AB to the Taxes Act 1988 having effect

for the purposes of section 121 of the Finance Act 1993 with the amendments made by this Schedule.

GENERAL NOTE

This paragraph preserves until 5 April 1999 the entitlement to in-year payments of tax credits relating to friendly societies' tax exempt business.

Schedule 19AC to the Taxes Act 1988

13   (1) Schedule 19AC to the Taxes Act 1988 (modification of Taxes Act 1988 in relation to overseas life insurance companies) shall be amended as follows.

(2) Paragraph 2 (which falls with the repeal of paragraph 5B(1) to (3)) shall cease to have effect.

(3) In paragraph 5(1) (which notionally inserts subsections (6A) and (6B) into section 76) the notionally inserted subsection (6B) shall cease to have effect.

(4) In paragraph 5A (which confers entitlement to tax credits on overseas life insurance companies) after sub-paragraph (2) there shall be inserted—

"(3) Nothing in this paragraph shall be taken to confer on an overseas life insurance company any entitlement to make a claim under section 231(3)."

(5) In paragraph 5B (which makes provision similar to section 242) sub-paragraphs (1) to (3) shall cease to have effect.

(6) For sub-paragraph (1) of paragraph 9 (which makes provision similar to section 434(1)) there shall be substituted—

"(1) In section 434, the following subsections shall be treated as inserted after subsection (1B)—

"(1C) The exclusion from section 11(2)(*a*), (*aa*) or (ab) of distributions received from companies resident in the United Kingdom shall not apply in relation to—

(*a*) the charge to corporation tax on the life assurance profits of an overseas life insurance company computed in accordance with the provisions of this Act applicable to Case I of Schedule D; or
(*b*) any computation of such profits in accordance with those provisions.

(1D) Paragraph 2 of Schedule F shall not have effect for the purposes of subsection (1C)(*a*) or (*b*) above, but this subsection shall not apply in relation to distributions in respect of which an overseas life insurance company is entitled to a tax credit under section 441A.

(1E) The reference in subsection (1C) above to the life assurance profits of an overseas life insurance company is a reference to the profits of the company—

(*a*) in respect of its life assurance business; or
(*b*) in respect of any category of life assurance business which it carries on."""

(7) Paragraph 9A (which falls with the repeal of section 434A(1)) shall cease to have effect.

(8) Sub-paragraph (1) of paragraph 10 (which notionally inserts into section 438 a provision similar to section 438(3) and (3AA)) shall cease to have effect.

(9) Sub-paragraph (2) of paragraph 10 (which notionally modifies subsections (6), (6A), (6D) and (6E) of section 438) shall cease to have effect.

(10) Paragraph 10A (which notionally inserts into section 439B a provision similar to section 439B(7)) shall cease to have effect.

(11) In paragraph 11A, sub-paragraph (1) (which notionally inserts into section 441A a provision similar to section 441A(1)) shall cease to have effect.

(12) Paragraph 12(1) (which falls with the repeal of paragraph 5B(1) to (3)) shall cease to have effect.

(13) In paragraph 15, sub-paragraph (1) (which falls with the repeal of paragraph 1(8) of Schedule 19AB) shall cease to have effect.

(14) Sub-paragraphs (2), (3), (5), (7), (9), (12) and (13) above have effect for accounting periods beginning on or after 2nd July 1997.

(15) Sub-paragraphs (4), (6), (8), (10) and (11) above have effect in relation to distributions made on or after 2nd July 1997.

(16) In determining, for the purposes of paragraph 5B(1) to (3) of Schedule 19AC to the Taxes Act 1988, the UK distribution income of an overseas life insurance company for an accounting period beginning before 2nd July 1997 and ending on or after that date, there shall be left out of account any distributions which are made on or after 2nd July 1997.

(17) In determining, for the purposes of subsections (6) to (7) of section 438 of the Taxes Act 1988 (as notionally amended by paragraph 10(2) of Schedule 19AC to that Act), the UK distribution income of, or foreign income dividends arising to, an overseas life insurance company for an accounting period beginning before 2nd July 1997 and ending on or after that date, there shall be left out of account any distributions which are made on or after 2nd July 1997.

GENERAL NOTE

This paragraph makes changes to rules about payment of tax credits on other non-pension distributions when relief for the insurance company's expenses of management or trading losses is set against them. This is to align with s 20 to this Act which withdraws this entitlement for companies generally for payments made on or after 2 July 1997. Other changes are made to the relief to which a life insurance company is entitled if it has been charged to tax on the "I minus E" basis and, as a consequence, its capacity to set ACT that it has paid on distributions that it has made against its mainstream corporation tax liability is less than it would have been if a company had been charged to tax on the trading profit from life assurance business. For accounting periods beginning on or after 1 January 1998 such relief can only be given by repayment or offset against corporation tax, and not by the payment of tax credits. The "I minus E" tax charge is based on the company's investment income and chargeable gains, less its expenses of management, and is intended to reflect the investment return that accrues for the benefit of policyholders as well as the company's trading profit.

Section 89 of the Finance Act 1989

14 (1) Section 89 of the Finance Act 1989 (policy holders' share of profits) shall be amended as follows.

(2) In subsection (2)—

(*a*) paragraph (*a*) (which provides for Case I profits to be reduced by unrelieved franked investment income in respect of which an election under section 438(6) has been made) shall cease to have effect;

(*b*) in paragraph (*b*) (which provides for Case I profits to be reduced by the shareholders' share of any other unrelieved franked investment income from investments held in connection with life assurance business)—

(i) the words "other unrelieved" shall cease to have effect; and
(ii) for "from investments held in connection with the company's life assurance business" there shall be substituted "which is referable to the company's basic life assurance and general annuity business"; and

(*c*) in paragraph (*c*) (which provides for Case I profits to be reduced by the shareholders' share of foreign income dividends in respect of such investments) for "in respect of investments held in connection with the company's life assurance business" there shall be substituted "which are referable to the company's basic life assurance and general annuity business".

(3) Subsection (8) (meaning of "unrelieved" franked investment income) shall cease to have effect.

(4) This paragraph has effect in relation to distributions made on or after 2nd July 1997.

Section 65 of the Finance (No 2) Act 1992

15 In section 65 of the Finance (No 2) Act 1992 (life assurance business: I minus E) in subsection (2) (meaning of relevant provisions) before paragraph (*a*) there shall be inserted—

"(*aa*)   section 434(1) and (1A) of the Taxes Act 1988 (section 208 not to apply in relation to life assurance profits computed in accordance with Case I of Schedule D etc);

(ab)   section 434(1C) and (1D) of the Taxes Act 1988 (which makes corresponding provision in relation to overseas life insurance companies and is notionally inserted by paragraph 9(1) of Schedule 19AC to that Act);".

Section 34   SCHEDULE 4

TAX CREDITS, TAXATION OF DISTRIBUTIONS ETC

GENERAL NOTE

This Schedule makes consequential amendments arising from the changes to the rate of tax credit and taxation of distributions. The amendments apply with effect from 6 April 1999 when those changes to the tax credits and taxation of distributions take effect.

The main changes are to remove entitlement to payment of tax credits, to reduce the rate of tax credit to 10 per cent, to reduce the rate of charge on such distributions to 10 per cent and to change the rate of charge for higher rate individuals and trustees. These changes will take effect for distributions made on or after 6 April 1999, the year of assessment 1999–2000.

PART I

GENERAL

THE TAXES MANAGEMENT ACT 1970

Section 7

1 (1) In section 7 of the Taxes Management Act 1970 (notice of liability to income tax and capital gains tax) in subsection (6) (sources of income which fall within that subsection) after the words "other than the basic rate" there shall be inserted ", the Schedule F ordinary rate".

(2) This paragraph has effect for the year 1999–00 and subsequent years of assessment.

GENERAL NOTE

Under TMA 1970 s 7(6), a person who is not liable to tax at a rate in excess of the lower or basic rates is not required to notify liability of income taxed at source or chargeable under Schedule F. This paragraph amends that provision to include a person who is not liable to tax at a rate in excess of the Schedule F ordinary rate for 1999–2000 and subsequent years.

Section 42 (pre-corporation tax self-assessment version)

2 (1) In section 42 of the Taxes Management Act 1970 (procedure for making claims), as it has effect in relation to corporation tax for accounting periods ending before the day appointed under section 199 of the Finance Act 1994, the following provisions shall cease to have effect—

(*a*) in subsection (5) (form of claim) the words "Subject to subsection (5A) below,";

(*b*) subsection (5A) (claims by companies for payment of tax credits); and

(*c*) subsection (10A) (extended meaning of terms used in subsection (5A)).

(2) This paragraph has effect in relation to tax credits in respect of distributions made on or after 6th April 1999.

GENERAL NOTE

No claim for payment of tax credit can be made in respect of company distributions made after 5 April 1999. The provisions in TMA 1970 s 42 governing such claims are no longer required and are repealed.

Section 42 (corporation tax self-assessment version)

3 (1) In section 42 of the Taxes Management Act 1970 (procedure for making claims), as it has effect in relation to corporation tax for accounting periods ending on or after the day appointed under section 199 of the Finance Act 1994, the following provisions shall cease to have effect—

(*a*) subsections (4) and (4A) (claims by companies for payment of tax credits); and

(*b*) in subsection (5), the words from "and the reference in subsection (4) above" onwards.

(2) This paragraph has effect in relation to tax credits in respect of distributions made on or after 6th April 1999.

GENERAL NOTE

No claim for payment of tax credit can be made in respect of company distributions made after 5 April 1999. The provisions in TMA 1970 s 42 governing such claims are no longer required and are repealed.

THE TAXES ACT 1988

Section 231

4 (1) In section 231 of the Taxes Act 1988 (tax credits for certain recipients of qualifying distributions) in subsection (1) (whose provisions are expressed to be subject to sections 247 and 441A) for "441A" there shall be substituted "469(2A)".

(2) This paragraph has effect in relation to distributions made on or after 6th April 1999.

GENERAL NOTE

This paragraph provides that an unauthorised unit trust is not entitled to a tax credit in respect of company distributions made after 5 April 1999 (see also para 12 below).

Section 232

5 (1) In section 232 of the Taxes Act 1988 (tax credits for non-UK residents) the following provisions shall cease to have effect—

(*a*) subsection (2) (funds to which section 615(2)(*b*) or (*c*) applies); and
(*b*) subsection (3) (sovereign powers, governments and international organisations).

(2) This paragraph has effect in relation to distributions made on or after 6th April 1999.

This paragraph provides that a foreign government or international organisation or a pension fund set up in the UK for employees of a foreign government is not entitled to a tax credit in respect of UK company distributions made after 5 April 1999.

Section 233

6 (1) Section 233 of the Taxes Act 1988 (taxation of certain recipients of distributions and in respect of non-qualifying distributions) shall be amended as follows.

(2) In subsections (1) to (1B), for the words "lower rate", wherever occurring, there shall be substituted "Schedule F ordinary rate".

(3) In subsection (1B), for the words "rate applicable to trusts", in both places where they occur, there shall be substituted "Schedule F trust rate".

(4) In subsection (2), in the definition of "excess liability", for "were charged at the lower rate to the exclusion of the higher rate or, as the case may be, the rate applicable to trusts" there shall be substituted

"were charged—

(*a*) in the case of income chargeable under Schedule F, at the Schedule F ordinary rate, and
(*b*) in the case of any other income, at the lower rate,

to the exclusion of the higher rate, the Schedule F upper rate or, as the case may be, the Schedule F trust rate".

(5) This paragraph has effect in relation to distributions made on or after 6th April 1999.

GENERAL NOTE

A non-qualifying distribution (eg a bonus issue of redeemable shares) made by a UK company does not carry a tax credit, but the recipient, other than a UK company, is treated as having paid tax at the lower rate (in the case of a trust, at the special trust rate) on the amount of the distribution. For such distributions made after 5 April 1999, the recipient is treated as having paid tax at the Schedule F ordinary rate (see s 31) (in the case of a trust, at the Schedule F trust rate (see s 32)).

The redemption of bonus shares constitutes a qualifying distribution. If the recipient of the redemption has paid tax in respect of "excess liability" on the issue of the shares, he is entitled to deduct the amount of that tax from any "excess liability" on the redemption. In respect of a distribution made after 5 April 1999, "excess liability" means the excess of the liability over what it would have been if all income were charged (as appropriate) at the Schedule F ordinary rate or the lower rate to the exclusion of tax at the higher rate, the Schedule F upper rate or the Schedule F trust rate.

Sections 235 to 237

7 (1) Sections 235 to 237 of the Taxes Act 1988 (distributions of exempt funds and bonus issues) shall cease to have effect.

(2) This paragraph has effect in relation to distributions made on or after 6th April 1999.

GENERAL NOTE

The anti-avoidance provisions in TA 1998 ss 235–237 denying repayment of tax credits on company distributions to certain shareholders will no longer be required and are repealed as regards distributions made after 5 April 1999.

Section 238

8 (1) In section 238(1) of the Taxes Act 1988 (interpretation etc) in the definition of "franked payment" for "rate of advance corporation tax" there shall be substituted "tax credit fraction".

(2) This paragraph has effect in relation to distributions made on or after 6th April 1999.

GENERAL NOTE

TA 1988 s 238(1) defines a franked payment as the amount of a qualifying distribution plus the corresponding amount of ACT. For distributions made after 5 April 1999, the definition is altered to the amount of the distribution plus the tax credit fraction (see s 30).

Section 241

9 (1) In section 241 of the Taxes Act 1988, for subsection (2) (amount on which ACT is payable where there is in an accounting period an excess of franked payments over franked investment income) there shall be substituted—

"(2) If in an accounting period there is such an excess, advance corporation tax shall be payable on the excess at nine-tenths of the rate of advance corporation tax."

(2) Sub-paragraph (1) above has effect in relation to accounting periods beginning on or after 6th April 1999.

(3) In the case of an accounting period beginning before, and ending on or after, 6th April 1999, the advance corporation tax payable shall be computed—

(*a*) in accordance with section 241, as amended by sub-paragraph (1) above, in the case of that part of the excess, if any, which, had there been such a period, would have accrued in an accounting period beginning with 6th April 1999 and ending with the true accounting period; and (*b*) in accordance with that section as it has effect apart from subsection (1) above in the case of that part of the excess, if any, which, had there been such a period, would have accrued in an accounting period beginning with the true accounting period and ending with 6th April 1999.

GENERAL NOTE

The rate of ACT (25 per cent of the distribution) is unchanged by the new provisions. However, where the company making a distribution receives franked investment income, it is necessary to introduce a new formula because the amounts of the franked payment and the franked investment income will be grossed up by reference to the tax credit fraction of 1/9th and not by reference to the rate of ACT.

For an accounting period beginning after 5 April 1999, the excess of franked payments over franked investment income received is charged to ACT at 9/10ths of the normal rate, ie at 22.5 per cent (sub-paras (1), (2)).

For an accounting period straddling 6 April 1999, the excess is to be calculated separately for the part of the period before 6 April 1999; the ACT on that excess is charged at 20 per cent. The excess for the part of the period after 5 April 1999 is charged at 22.5 per cent (sub-para (3)).

Section 249

10 (1) Section 249 of the Taxes Act 1988 (stock dividends treated as income) shall be amended as follows.

(2) In subsection (4) (taxation of individuals)—

(*a*) in the words preceding paragraph (*a*), for "lower rate" there shall be substituted "Schedule F ordinary rate";

(*b*) in paragraph (*a*), for "lower rate" there shall be substituted "Schedule F ordinary rate"; and

(*c*) in paragraph (*c*) after "as if it were income to which section 1A applies" there shall be inserted "as it applies to income chargeable under Schedule F".

(3) In subsection (6) (taxation of trustees) in paragraph (*b*) for "lower rate" there shall be substituted "Schedule F ordinary rate".

(4) This paragraph has effect in relation to share capital, within the meaning of section 249 of the Taxes Act 1988, issued on or after 6th April 1999.

GENERAL NOTE

Where a UK company issues shares which constitute a stock dividend after 5 April 1999 to an individual or to a trustee, the recipient will be treated as having received income of an amount equal to the "appropriate amount in cash" grossed up at the Schedule F ordinary rate. The "appropriate amount in cash" is the cash dividend foregone or the market value of the shares issued.

Section 421

11 (1) In section 421 of the Taxes Act 1988 (taxation of borrower when loan under s 419 released etc) in subsection (1)—

(*a*) in paragraphs (*a*) and (*b*) for the words "lower rate", in both places where they occur, there shall be substituted "Schedule F ordinary rate"; and

(*b*) in paragraph (*c*), after the words "as if it were income to which section 1A applies" there shall be inserted "by virtue of subsection (2)(*b*) of that section".

(2) This paragraph has effect in relation to the release or writing off of the whole or part of a debt on or after 6th April 1999.

GENERAL NOTE

If a close company makes a loan to a participator and subsequently releases or writes off the debt, the participator is treated as having received income of an amount equal to the amount written off after deduction of tax at the lower rate of income tax. Where the writing off takes place after 5 April 1999 the amount is deemed to have been received after deduction of tax at the Schedule F ordinary rate.

Section 469

12   (1) Section 469 of the Taxes Act 1988 (unit trusts other than authorised unit trusts) shall be amended as follows.

(2) In subsection (2) (income of the trustees to which section 1A applies to be chargeable at the basic rate instead of the lower rate) for "lower rate" there shall be substituted "rate applicable in accordance with subsection (1A) of that section".

(3) After subsection (2) there shall be inserted—

"(2A) Section 231(1) shall not apply where the recipient of the distribution there mentioned is the trustees of the scheme.

(2B) Section 233(1) shall not apply where the person there mentioned is the trustees of the scheme."

(4) In subsection (9) (sections 686 and 687 not to apply) after "686" there shall be inserted ", 686A".

(5) This paragraph has effect in relation to distributions made on or after 6th April 1999.

GENERAL NOTE

Where the trustees of an unauthorised unit trust receive savings income (including distributions from UK companies) they are chargeable to income tax at the basic rate. For distributions received after 5 April 1999 the charge will continue to be at the basic rate (and not the Schedule F ordinary rate) but the trustees will not be entitled to a tax credit and will not be treated as having paid any tax on the distribution. The new provisions regarding qualifying distributions received by trustees (TA 1988 s 686A introduced by s 32 above) will not apply to the trustees of an unauthorised unit trust.

Section 549

13 (1) In section 549 of the Taxes Act 1988 (policies of life insurance etc: corresponding deficiency relief) in subsection (2) (which contains a definition of "excess liability")—

(*a*) after "(so far as applicable in accordance with section 1A) the lower rate" there shall be inserted "or the Schedule F ordinary rate"; and

(*b*) for "any higher rate" there shall be substituted "the higher rate and the Schedule F upper rate".

(2) This paragraph has effect for the year 1999–00 and subsequent years of assessment.

GENERAL NOTE

Where an individual has been taxed on a gain from a life assurance policy, he may be entitled to relief from higher rate tax if there is no overall gain when the policy ends. For 1999–2000 and subsequent years the relief may be given against the Schedule F upper rate.

Section 660C

14 (1) Section 660C of the Taxes Act 1988 (settlements where the settlor retains an interest: nature of the charge on settlor) shall be amended as follows.

(2) In subsection (1) (tax to be charged under Case VI of Schedule D) for "under Case VI of Schedule D" there shall be substituted—

"(*a*) in the case of income falling within subsection (1A) below, as if it were income to which section 1A applies by virtue of subsection (2)(*b*) of that section; and

(*b*) in the case of any other income, under Case VI of Schedule D".

(3) After subsection (1) there shall be inserted—

"(1A) Income falls within this subsection if it is—

(*a*) income chargeable under Schedule F;

(*b*) income to which section 1A applies by virtue of its being equivalent foreign income falling within subsection (3)(*b*) of that section and chargeable under Case V of Schedule D;

(*c*) a distribution in relation to which section 233(1) applies;

(*d*) a qualifying distribution whose amount or value is determined in accordance with section 233(1A);

(*e*) a non-qualifying distribution, within the meaning of section 233(1B);

(*f*) income treated as arising by virtue of section 249;

(*g*) income treated as received by virtue of section 421(1)(*a*)."

(4) This paragraph has effect for the year 1999–00 and subsequent years of assessment.

GENERAL NOTE

Where income of a settlement is deemed to be the income of the settlor it is currently charged under Schedule D Case VI. For 1999–2000 and subsequent years the charge will be at the Schedule F ordinary rate and the Schedule F upper rate where appropriate in respect of —

(*a*) qualifying distributions and equivalent foreign income;
(*b*) non-qualifying distributions;
(*c*) stock dividends; and
(*d*) loans from close companies written off.

Other types of income will continue to be charged under Schedule D Case VI.

Section 687

15 (1) In section 687 of the Taxes Act 1988 (payments under discretionary trusts) subsection (3) (amounts which may be set against the amount assessable on trustees) shall be amended as follows.

(2) For paragraphs (*a*) and (*aa*) there shall be substituted—

"(*a*) the amount of any tax on income arising to the trustees which (not being income the tax on which falls within paragraphs (a1) to (bc) below) is charged in pursuance of section 686 at the rate applicable to trusts or the Schedule F trust rate;
(a1) the amount of tax at a rate equal to the difference between the Schedule F ordinary rate and the Schedule F trust rate on any income of the trustees chargeable under Schedule F;
(a2) the amount of tax which, by virtue of section 233(1A), is charged, at a rate equal to the difference between the Schedule F ordinary rate and the Schedule F trust rate, on the amount or value of the whole or any part of any qualifying distribution included in the income arising to the trustees;
(*aa*) the amount of tax which, by virtue of section 233(1B), is charged, at a rate equal to the difference between the Schedule F ordinary rate and the Schedule F trust rate, on the amount or value of the whole or any part of any non-qualifying distribution included in the income arising to the trustees;".

(3) For paragraph (*b*) there shall be substituted—

"(*b*) the amount of tax at a rate equal to the difference between the Schedule F ordinary rate and the Schedule F trust rate on any sum treated, under section 249(6), as income of the trustees;".

(4) After paragraph (*b*) there shall be inserted—

"(*bb*) the amount of tax at a rate equal to the difference between the Schedule F ordinary rate and the Schedule F trust rate on any sum treated under section 421(1)(*a*) as income of the trustees;
(bc) the amount of tax at a rate equal to the difference between the Schedule F ordinary rate and the Schedule F trust rate on any sum treated under section 686A as income of the trustees;".

(5) This paragraph has effect for the year 1999–00 and subsequent years of assessment.

GENERAL NOTE

Where the trustees of a discretionary settlement make a distribution to a beneficiary in the exercise of a discretion, the beneficiary is treated as having received the amount of the distribution after deduction of tax at the special trust rate. The trustees are assessed on the amount of the notional tax deducted, subject to set-off of the difference between tax at the special trust rate and the lower rate where the income consists of—

(*a*) a non-qualifying distribution; or
(*b*) a foreign income dividend; or
(*c*) a stock dividend.

A set-off of tax at the special trust rate may be made in respect of other sources of income (TA 1988 s 687(3)).

For 1999–2000 and subsequent years, the amounts to be set off will be at the difference between the Schedule F trust rate and the lower rate in the case of income under heads (*a*)–(*c*) and also where the income consists of—

(*d*) other income chargeable under Schedule F; or
(*e*) the writing off of a loan from a close company; or
(*f*) a distribution made by a company on the redemption, repayment or purchase of its own shares or on the purchase of rights to acquire its own shares (TA 1988 s 686A inserted by s 32(9) above).

In the .case of other income chargeable under Schedule F, the set-off will be at the special trust rate or the Schedule F trust rate as appropriate.

Section 689B

16 (1) Section 689B of the Taxes Act 1988 (order in which expenses of trustees are to be set against income) shall be amended as follows.

(2) In subsection (1)—

(*a*) in paragraph (*a*) (set against income within subsection (2) or (3) before other income) after "subsection (2)" there shall be inserted ", (2A)";
(*b*) in paragraph (*b*) (set against income within subsection (2) before subsection (3)) after "subsection (2)" there shall be inserted "or (2A)"; and
(*c*) at the end of paragraph (*b*) there shall be added

"and
(*c*) as set against so much (if any) of any income as is income falling within subsection (2) below before being set against income falling within subsection (2A) below".

(3) In subsection (2) (income against which expenses are to be first set)—

(*a*) before paragraph (*a*) there shall be inserted—

"(*za*) so much of the income of the trustees as is income chargeable under Schedule F;"; and

(*b*) after paragraph (*a*) there shall be inserted—

"(*aa*) so much of the income of the trustees as is a non-qualifying distribution, within the meaning of section 233(1B);".

(4) After subsection (2) there shall be inserted—

"(2A) Income falls within this subsection if it is income to which section 1A applies by virtue of its being equivalent foreign income falling within subsection (3)(*b*) of that section and chargeable under Case V of Schedule D.''

(5) In subsection (3) (income to which section 1A applies but which does not fall within subsection (2) of s 689B) after ''subsection (2)'' there shall be inserted ''or (2A)''.

(6) This paragraph has effect for the year 1999–00 and subsequent years of assessment.

GENERAL NOTE

This paragraph amends the order in which management expenses of a settlement are to be set off against income chargeable on the trustees for 1999–2000 and subsequent years. The order of set-off is—

(1) Against—

    (*a*) income chargeable under Schedule F;
    (*b*) qualifying distributions received by non-resident trustees;
    (*c*) foreign income dividends;
    (*d*) stock dividends.

(2) Against equivalent foreign income falling within TA 1988 s 1A(3)(*b*).

(3) Against other income falling within TA 1988 s 1A not included in (1) or (2) above.

(4) Against other income not included in (1)–(3) above.

Section 699

17 (1) In section 699 of the Taxes Act 1988 (relief from higher rate tax for inheritance tax on accrued income) in subsection (2) (definition of ''excess liability'')—

    (*a*) after ''(so far as applicable in accordance with section 1A) the lower rate'' there shall be inserted ''or the Schedule F ordinary rate''; and
    (*b*) for ''any higher rate'' there shall be substituted ''the higher rate and the Schedule F upper rate''.

(2) This paragraph has effect for the year 1999–00 and subsequent years of assessment.

GENERAL NOTE

TA 1988 s 699 provides relief from higher rate tax where IHT has been paid on accrued income. For 1999–2000 and subsequent years, higher rate tax includes the Schedule F upper rate.

Section 703

18 (1) In section 703 of the Taxes Act 1988 (cancellation of tax advantage) in subsection (5)(*b*) (which requires a notice under that section to specify the amount equal to tax at the lower rate on the amount there mentioned) for ''lower rate'' there shall be substituted ''Schedule F ordinary rate''.

(2) This paragraph has effect for the year 1999–00 and subsequent years of assessment.

GENERAL NOTE

When a tax advantage is counteracted under TA 1988 s 703 by deeming a taxpayer to have received a distribution from a company, the Revenue may deem the company to have paid ACT on that distribution. If so, they must issue a notice to the company specifying the amount of tax at the lower rate which the taxpayer has paid. For 1999–2000 and subsequent years, the notice will show the amount of tax at the Schedule F ordinary rate.

Section 709

19 (1) In section 709 of the Taxes Act 1988 (meaning of tax advantage etc) in subsection (2A) (references to a relief and to repayment of tax to include references to a tax credit and payment of any amount in respect of a tax credit) the words "and to a repayment of tax", "respectively" and "and to a payment of any amount in respect of a tax credit" shall be omitted.

(2) This paragraph has effect for the year 1999–00 and subsequent years of assessment.

GENERAL NOTE

The definition of a tax advantage in TA 1988 s 709 is amended to exclude for 1999–2000 and subsequent years a reference to repayment of tax credits.

Section 743

20 (1) Section 743 of the Taxes Act 1988 (provisions supplemental to section 739 etc) shall be amended as follows.

(2) In subsection (1) (subject to an exception for income which has borne tax by deduction at the basic rate or the lower rate, income chargeable under s 739 to be charged under Case VI of Schedule D)—

(a) for "or the lower rate" there shall be substituted ", the lower rate or the Schedule F ordinary rate"; and

(b) for "under Case VI of Schedule D" there shall be substituted—

"(a) in the case of income falling within subsection (1A) below, as if it were income to which section 1A applies by virtue of paragraph (2)(b) of that section; and

(b) in the case of any other income, under Case VI of Schedule D".

(3) After subsection (1) there shall be inserted—

"(1A) Income falls within this subsection if it is—

(a) income chargeable under Schedule F;

(b) income to which section 1A applies by virtue of its being equivalent foreign income falling within subsection (3)(b) of that section and chargeable under Case V of Schedule D;

(c) a distribution in relation to which section 233(1) applies;

(*d*) a qualifying distribution whose amount or value is determined in accordance with section 233(1A);

(*e*) a non-qualifying distribution, within the meaning of section 233(1B);

(*f*) income treated as arising by virtue of section 249;

(*g*) income treated as received by virtue of section 421(1)(*a*)."

(4) This paragraph has effect for the year 1999–00 and subsequent years of assessment.

GENERAL NOTE

TA 1988 ss 739, 743 provide that a tax advantage obtained by transferring assets abroad shall be countered by deeming the transferor to be in receipt of income chargeable to UK tax under Schedule D Case VI except to the extent that it has borne tax at the lower or basic rate. For 1999–2000 and subsequent years the exception is extended to tax at the Schedule F ordinary rate, and income of the following kinds is chargeable under Schedule F and not Schedule D Case VI—

(*a*) income which is within Schedule F and equivalent foreign income;

(*b*) a company distribution which does not carry a tax credit;

(c) a qualifying distribution whose value is determined by TA 1988 s 233(1A);

(*d*) a non-qualifying distribution;

(*e*) a stock dividend; and

(*f*) the writing off of a loan from a close company.

Section 819

21 (1) In section 819 of the Taxes Act 1988 (old references to standard rate tax) in subsection (2)—

(*a*) after "(so far as applicable in accordance with section 1A) the lower rate" there shall be inserted "or the Schedule F ordinary rate"; and

(*b*) for "any higher rate" there shall be substituted "the higher rate and the Schedule F upper rate".

(2) This paragraph has effect for the year 1999–00 and subsequent years of assessment.

GENERAL NOTE

The definition of income not chargeable at the higher rate in TA 1988 s 819 is amended for 1999–2000 and subsequent years—

(*a*) to apply to income chargeable at the Schedule F upper rate; and

(*b*) to include income chargeable at the Schedule F ordinary rate.

Section 832

22 (1) In section 832 of the Taxes Act 1988 (interpretation of the Tax Acts) the following definitions shall be inserted in subsection (1) at the appropriate places—

(*a*) """the Schedule F ordinary rate" shall be construed in accordance with section 1B(2);'';

(*b*) """the Schedule F trust rate" shall be construed in accordance with section 686(1A);";
(*c*) """the Schedule F upper rate" shall be construed in accordance with section 1B(2);".

(2) This paragraph has effect for the year 1999–00 and subsequent years of assessment.

Schedule 13

23 (1) Schedule 13 to the Taxes Act 1988 (collection of ACT) shall be amended as follows.

(2) In paragraph 2, in sub-paragraph (4) (calculation of amount to be paid where the franked payments for the return period exceed the franked investment income or where there is no franked investment income) for the words following "shall be calculated" there shall be substituted "in accordance with sub-paragraph (4A) below".

(3) After that sub-paragraph there shall be inserted—

"(4A) The tax mentioned in sub-paragraph (4) above shall be calculated at a rate equal to nine-tenths of the rate of advance corporation tax in force for the financial year in which the return period ends—

(*a*) in a case falling within paragraph (*a*) of that sub-paragraph, on the excess mentioned in that paragraph, or
(*b*) in a case falling within paragraph (*b*) of that sub-paragraph, on the amount shown under sub-paragraph (1)(*a*) above."

(4) In paragraph 4 (receipt of franked investment income after payment of ACT) for sub-paragraph (3) (which imposes a limit on repayment) there shall be substituted—

"(3) The amount of the repayment—

(*a*) if no franked payments were made by the company in the return period for which a return is made by virtue of sub-paragraph (2) above, shall not exceed an amount equal to the advance corporation tax that would be payable in respect of a distribution equal to the difference between—

(i) the franked investment income received, and
(ii) the tax credit comprised in that franked investment income; and

(*b*) in any other case, shall not exceed an amount equal to the advance corporation tax that would be payable in respect of a distribution equal to the amount by which—

(i) the franked investment income received, exceeds
(ii) the franked payments made in the return period,

at the rate provided in paragraph 2(4A) above."

(5) The preceding provisions of this paragraph have effect in relation to return periods, within the meaning of Schedule 13 to the Taxes Act 1988, ending on or after 6th April 1999.

(6) If, in the period beginning with 1st April 1999 and ending with 5th April 1999—

  (a) any franked investment income is received by a company, or
  (b) any franked payments are made by a company,

that period shall, in the case of the company, be treated for the purposes of Schedule 13 to the Taxes Act 1988 as if it were a separate return period.

THE TAXATION OF CHARGEABLE GAINS ACT 1992

Section 4

24 (1) Section 4 of the Taxation of Chargeable Gains Act 1992 (rates of capital gains tax) shall be amended as follows.

(2) In subsection (2) (case where income tax is chargeable at the higher rate on part of income of an individual) after "the higher rate", where first occurring, there shall be inserted "or the Schedule F upper rate".

(3) In subsection (3) (case where income tax is not chargeable at the higher rate on income of an individual but his gains exceed the unused basic rate band) after "the higher rate", where first occurring, there shall be inserted "or the Schedule F upper rate".

(4) In subsection (3A) (disregard of income chargeable at the lower rate in accordance with section 1A of the Taxes Act 1988 etc)—

  (a) after "the lower rate" there shall be inserted "or the Schedule F ordinary rate"; and
  (b) after "the higher rate" there shall be inserted "or the Schedule F upper rate".

(5) In subsection (3B), in paragraph (a) (determination in certain cases of the amount of income comprised in an individual's total income which is chargeable at the higher rate) after "the higher rate" there shall be inserted "or the Schedule F upper rate".

(6) This paragraph has effect for the year of assessment 1999–00 and subsequent years of assessment.

Section 6

25 (1) In section 6 of the Taxation of Chargeable Gains Act 1992 (other special cases) in subsection (3) (cases where income includes gains on policies of life insurance etc) in paragraph (b) after "as if no income were chargeable at the higher rate" there shall be inserted "or the Schedule F upper rate".

(2) This paragraph has effect for the year of assessment 1999–00 and subsequent years of assessment.

GENERAL NOTE

Paragraphs 13–25 contain consequential amendments to ensure that income is charged to tax at the new Schedule F rates of tax.

PART II

INSURANCE COMPANIES AND LLOYD'S UNDERWRITERS

THE TAXES ACT 1988

Section 231B

26 (1) In section 231B of the Taxes Act 1988 in subsection (4)(*b*), the words "or 441A(7)" shall be omitted.

(2) This paragraph has effect in relation to distributions made on or after 6th April 1999.

Section 434

27 (1) In section 434 of the Taxes Act 1988 (franked investment income etc) in subsection (1A) (which modifies paragraph 2 of Schedule F) the words from "but this subsection" onwards shall cease to have effect.

(2) This paragraph has effect in relation to distributions made on or after 6th April 1999.

Section 441A

28 (1) In section 441A, subsections (2) to (8) (regulations about tax credits to which insurance companies are entitled) shall cease to have effect.

(2) This paragraph has effect in relation to distributions made on or after 6th April 1999.

Schedule 19AC

29 (1) Schedule 19AC to the Taxes Act 1988 (overseas life insurance companies) shall be amended as follows.

(2) In paragraph 9(1) (which notionally inserts subsections (1C) to (1E) into section 434 of the Taxes Act 1988) in the notionally inserted subsection (1D), the words from "but this subsection" onwards shall cease to have effect.

(3) Paragraph 11A(2) (which modifies section 441A(2) and (3) of the Taxes Act 1988) shall cease to have effect.

(4) This paragraph has effect in relation to distributions made on or after 6th April 1999.

GENERAL NOTE

Paragraphs 26–29 remove an insurance company's entitlement to tax credits paid to it on dividends and other distributions derived from shares that support its overseas life assurance business.

THE FINANCE ACT 1993

Schedule 20

30 (1) In Schedule 20 to the Finance Act 1993 (Lloyd's underwriters: special reserve funds) the following provisions shall cease to have effect—

(*a*) paragraph 9(3) (claims for payment of tax credits); and

(*b*) in paragraph 11(3)(*c*) (value of fund as increased by tax repayment or tax credit received under paragraph 9(2) or (3)) the words "or tax credit received" and "or (3)".

(2) Sub-paragraph (1) above has effect in relation to distributions made on or after 6th April 1999.

GENERAL NOTE

This paragraph removes the entitlement to have credits paid on dividends and other distributions derived from shares that are held in special reserve funds at Lloyd's.

SCHEDULE 5

LIMITATION OF ENTITLEMENT TO RELIEF UNDER SECTION 35

GENERAL NOTE

This Schedule sets out circumstances in which payment of transitional relief to charities for 1999–2000 to 2003–04 is not to be made. Part I (paras 1–5) applies to a charity which holds 10 per cent or more of the class of shares etc in respect of which the distribution is made. Part II (paras 6–8) applies to bonus issues of shares.

CHARITY HOLDING 10 PER CENT OF SHARES

Before the repeal of TA 1988 ss 235, 236 by Sch 8 para 9 of this Act, a charity owning at least 10 per cent of the relevant class of shares in a company from which it received a distribution was not entitled to payment of a tax credit in respect of that distribution unless either—

(*a*) the distribution was made out of profits of the company arising after the relevant shares were acquired; or

(*b*) the relevant shares were acquired before 6 April 1965.

Unless the conditions in (*a*) or (*b*) are satisfied, such a charity will not be entitled to payment of the transitional relief; the provisions of TA 1988 s 236 continue to apply for this purpose despite its repeal for other purposes (paras 1, 2, 4).

This provision does not apply to a bonus issue of shares which is treated as a distribution, for which there are separate provisions in paras 6, 7 below (para 3).

BONUS ISSUES

For this purpose, a bonus issue means—

(*a*) a distribution in excess of new consideration received (TA 1988 s 209(3)); or

(*b*) a bonus issue following a repayment of share capital (TA 1988 s 210); or

(*c*) a payment not treated as a repayment of share capital (TA 1988 s 211(1)).

A charity which receives a bonus issue will not be entitled to payment of transitional relief (para 6), except where, if the issue had been declared as a dividend it would have represented a normal return on the consideration paid for the shares in respect of which the bonus issue was made (or for shares from which those shares derived) (para 7). Where the consideration for the acquisition of the shares was in excess of market value, or if no consideration was provided, market value at the time of acquisition is to be taken. In considering whether an amount exceeds a normal return, regard is to be had to the length of time for which the shares have been held and the amounts of any distributions made since the time of acquisition (para 8).

PART I

QUALIFYING DISTRIBUTIONS OTHER THAN BONUS ISSUES

GENERAL NOTE

This Part limits the entitlement to relief for claimants under s 35(1) in respect of certain qualifying distributions.

1 This Part of this Schedule applies where a person ("the claimant")—

(*a*) would, apart from paragraph 2 below, be entitled to a payment under section 35(1) of this Act in respect of a distribution, and

(*b*) his holding (together with any associated holding) of any one class of the shares, securities or rights by virtue of which he is entitled to the distribution amounts to not less than 10 per cent of that class.

GENERAL NOTE

This paragraph provides that it applies where the claimant is entitled to 10 per cent or more of the distribution on any class of shares, securities or rights by reason of its holdings (together with any associated holding) of those shares, securities or rights.

2 Where this Part of this Schedule applies, if any part of the distribution is not a part—

(*a*) to which profits arising after the date of acquisition are attributable in accordance with section 236 of the Taxes Act 1988, or

(*b*) in relation to which the date of acquisition is earlier than 6th April 1965,

then no payment under section 35(1) of this Act shall be made to the claimant in respect of the distribution.

GENERAL NOTE

This paragraph denies the claim for relief if any part of the distribution relates to acquisitions on or after 6 April 1965 or is attributable under TA 1988 s 236 to profits on or before the date of acquisition of those shares, securities or rights. Section 235 currently restricts the exemption from tax where the distribution relates to profits arising on or before the date of acquisition under s 236 in certain circumstances.

3 This Part of this Schedule applies to any qualifying distribution except any amount which is treated as such in accordance with section 209(3) or sections 210 and 211 of the Taxes Act 1988.

GENERAL NOTE

This paragraph provides that the claim is denied in respect of any qualifying distribution except those with TA 1988 ss 209(3), 210 and 211, "a bonus issue" which is dealt with by Part II.

4 Notwithstanding the repeal of sections 235 and 236 of the Taxes Act 1988 by this Act, section 236 of the Taxes Act 1988 as it applies in relation to distributions made before 6th April 1999 shall continue to apply for the purposes of this Part of this Schedule as it applies for the purposes of section 235 of the Taxes Act 1988 in relation to such distributions.

GENERAL NOTE

This paragraph provides that the test in TA 1988 s 236 is still applicable for distributions made after 6 April 1999. This amendment is necessary as ss 235–237 are repealed for distributions made on or after 6 April 1999 by Sch 4 para 7.

5 For the purposes of this Part of this Schedule and section 236 of the Taxes Act 1988 as it applies by virtue of paragraph 4 above, the date of acquisition, in relation to any part of a distribution or profits attributable to it, is the date on which the shares, securities or rights by virtue of which a person is entitled to that part were acquired by him.

PART II
BONUS ISSUES

GENERAL NOTE

This Part similarly limits the entitlement to relief under s 35(1) in respect of "a bonus issue".

6 A person ("the claimant") who receives an amount treated as a distribution by virtue of section 209(3), 210 or 211(1) of the Taxes Act 1988 ("a bonus issue") shall not be entitled to a payment under section 35(1) of this Act in respect of that distribution, except to the extent that paragraph 7 below otherwise provides.

GENERAL NOTE

This paragraph provides that no such relief is available to the claimant except where para 7 applies. For this purpose " a bonus issue" is a distribution by virtue of TA 1988 ss 209(3), 210 or 211(1).

7 Paragraph 6 above shall not affect a person's entitlement to a payment under section 35 of this Act in respect of that part (if any) of a bonus issue made in respect of any shares or securities which, if it had been declared as a dividend, would represent a normal return to the claimant—

(*a*) on the consideration provided by him for the relevant shares or securities, that is to say, those in respect of which the bonus issue was made; and

(*b*) if the relevant shares or securities are derived from shares or securities previously acquired by the claimant, on the shares or securities which were previously acquired.

GENERAL NOTE

This paragraph provides that para 6 does not restrict the relief under s 35(1) in respect of any part of a bonus issue which if it had been a dividend would represent a normal return on the consideration for the relevant shares or securities (or the shares or securities from which they were derived). The relevant shares or securities are those in respect of which the bonus issue is made.

8   For the purposes of paragraph 7 above—

(*a*) if the consideration provided by the claimant for any of the relevant shares or securities was in excess of their market value at the time he acquired them, or if no consideration was provided by him for any of the relevant shares or securities, the claimant shall be taken to have provided for those shares or securities consideration equal to their market value at the time he acquired them; and

(*b*) in determining whether an amount received by way of dividend exceeds a normal return, regard shall be had to the length of time previous to the receipt of that amount since the claimant first acquired any of the relevant shares or securities and to any dividends and other distributions made in respect of them during that time.

GENERAL NOTE

For the purposes of para 7 this paragraph provides that where the consideration for any of the relevant shares or securities was above their then market value, or nil, then the consideration is deemed to be the market value at the time of acquisition. In determining whether the dividend exceeds a normal return, consideration is given to the length of any holding and other distributions received.

SCHEDULE 6

FOREIGN INCOME DIVIDENDS

Section 13 of the Taxes Act 1988

1 (1) Section 13 of the Taxes Act 1988 (small companies' relief) shall be amended as follows.

(2) In subsection (7) (profits of a company for an accounting period to include foreign income dividends) the words "and with the addition of foreign income dividends arising to the company" shall cease to have effect.

(3) Subsection (8A) (definition of "foreign income dividends") shall cease to have effect.

(4) This paragraph has effect for accounting periods beginning on or after 6th April 1999.

SMALL COMPANIES RATE

This paragraph amends TA 1988 s 13 to remove references to FIDs, currently taken into account in s 13(7) in determining the level of profits, in respect of accounting periods ("APs") commencing after 5 April 1999.

Section 75 of the Taxes Act 1988

2 (1) Section 75 of the Taxes Act 1988 (expenses of management: investment companies) shall be amended as follows.

(2) In subsection (2) (deductions from amount treated as expenses of management) the words "foreign income dividends" shall cease to have effect.

(3) Subsection (6) (definition of "foreign income dividends") shall cease to have effect.

(4) This paragraph has effect in relation to distributions made on or after 6th April 1999.

RELIEF FOR EXPENSES OF MANAGEMENT

This paragraph makes a similar change to TA 1988 s 75 by removing references to FIDs in the types of non-taxable income which do not have to be offset against management expenses in determining relief available to investment companies.

Chapter VA of Part VI of the Taxes Act 1988

3 (1) Sections 246A to 246Y of the Taxes Act 1988 (foreign income dividends) shall cease to have effect.

(2) The repeal of sections 246A to 246E and 246G of the Taxes Act 1988 has effect in relation to distributions made on or after 6th April 1999.

(3) The repeal of sections 246F, 246H to 246J and 246N to 246Y of the Taxes Act 1988 has effect for accounting periods beginning on or after 6th April 1999.

(4) The repeal of sections 246K to 246M of the Taxes Act 1988 has effect for accounting periods of the parent (within the meaning of those sections) beginning on or after 6th April 1999.

REPEAL OF FID LEGISLATION

Sub-paragraph (1) provides for the basic repeal of the FID legislation and then sub-paras (2)–(4) set out the commencement dates.

Sub-paragraph (2) disapplies the provisions dealing with elections (TA 1988 ss 246A and B), the provisions dealing with tax treatment of recipients (ss 246C–E), and the shareholder information provisions (in s 246G) in respect of post-5 April 1999 distributions.

Sub-paragraph (3) disapplies the provisions reducing ACT due on FIDs by reference to FIDs received (s 246F), the Revenue information provision (s 246H), preliminary calculation provisions (ss 246H–J), repayment and offset provisions (ss 246N–R), IHC provisions (ss 246S–V) and supplementary provisions (ss 246W–Y) for APs beginning on or after 6 April 1999.

Sub-paragraph (4) repeals the provisions whereby FIDs of a parent company can be matched against overseas profits of subsidiaries (ss 246K–M) in respect of APs of the *parent* commencing after 5 April 1999.

Section 247 of the Taxes Act 1988

4 (1) In section 247 of the Taxes Act 1988 (dividends etc paid by one member of a group to another) subsections (5A) to (5D) (which relate to foreign income dividends) shall cease to have effect.

(2) This paragraph has effect in relation to distributions made on or after 6th April 1999.

DEEMED FIDS: GROUP INCOME ELECTIONS

This paragraph repeals TA 1988 ss 247(5A)–(5D) (provisions introduced consequent upon the introduction of FA 1997 Sch 7 to enable deemed FIDs to be paid within a group income dividend election) with effect from 6 April 1999.

Section 431 of the Taxes Act 1988

5 (1) In section 431(2) of the Taxes Act 1988 (interpretation of Chapter I of Part XII) the definition of "foreign income dividends" shall cease to have effect.

(2) This paragraph has effect for accounting periods beginning on or after 6th April 1999.

INSURANCE COMPANIES

This paragraph removes a reference to FIDs from TA 1988 s 431(2), and para 6 removes spent references to FIDs in s 434 in either case for APs commencing after 5 April 1999. Paragraph 7 removes a similarly spent reference in s 458 to FIDs in respect of post-5 April 1999 distributions.

Section 434 of the Taxes Act 1988

6 (1) Section 434 of the Taxes Act 1988 (franked investment income etc) shall be amended as follows.

(2) Subsections (3B) to (3D) (which relate to foreign income dividends) shall cease to have effect.

(3) In subsection (6A), paragraphs (*aa*) to (ac) (which define expressions used in subsections (3B) to (3D)) shall cease to have effect.

(4) This paragraph has effect for accounting periods beginning on or after 6th April 1999.

Section 458 of the Taxes Act 1988

7 (1) In section 458 of the Taxes Act 1988 (capital redemption business) in subsection (2) (certain foreign income dividends treated as part of profits in ascertaining loss) the words "and foreign income dividends arising to" shall cease to have effect.

(2) This paragraph has effect in relation to distributions made on or after 6th April 1999.

Chapter III of Part XII of the Taxes Act 1988

8 (1) In section 468H of the Taxes Act 1988 (interpretation of sections 468I to 468R)—

  (*a*) subsection (5) (construction of references to foreign income dividends) shall cease to have effect; and

  (*b*) in subsection (6), for "to 468R" there shall be substituted "to 468Q".

(2) In section 468I of the Taxes Act 1988 (distribution accounts)—

  (*a*) in subsection (2), the words "which are not foreign income dividends" shall cease to have effect; and

  (*b*) subsections (3), (5), (5A) and (7) shall cease to have effect.

(3) In section 468J of the Taxes Act 1988 (dividend distributions)—

  (*a*) in subsection (1), the words "or a part of the total amount" and "which are not foreign income dividends" shall cease to have effect;

  (*b*) in subsection (2), the words "or, as the case may be, the part" shall cease to have effect; and

  (*c*) subsection (3) shall cease to have effect.

(4) Section 468K of the Taxes Act 1988 (foreign income distributions) shall cease to have effect.

(5) In section 468M of the Taxes Act 1988 (deduction of tax: simple case) in subsection (5) (definition of "eligible income") paragraph (*c*) shall cease to have effect.

(6) In section 468Q of the Taxes Act 1988 (dividend distribution to corporate unit holder)—

  (*a*) in subsection (2)(*a*), the words "a foreign income distribution" shall cease to have effect;

  (*b*) in subsection (3)—

(i) for the formula there shall be substituted the following formula—

$$U = \frac{A \times C}{D}$$

(ii) the definition of "B" shall cease to have effect; and

(c) subsection (4) shall cease to have effect.

(7) Section 468R of the Taxes Act 1988 (foreign income distribution to corporate holder) shall cease to have effect.

(8) Sub-paragraphs (1)(a), (5) and (6) above have effect for distribution periods beginning on or after 6th April 1999.

(9) Sub-paragraphs (1)(b), (2) to (4) and (7) above have effect for distribution periods the distribution date for which falls on or after 6th April 1999.

AUTHORISED UNIT TRUSTS

Consequent upon the abolition of the FID regime, this paragraph removes definition provisions in TA 1988 s 468H, the provisions in s 468I and in s 468J and s 468K in its entirety dealing with FID and non FID distributions, and references to FIDs in s 468M. It also substitutes a new formula in s 468Q(3)—dividends to corporate holders of units in AUTs—and repeals s 468R (which deals with FID distributions to such holders). As appropriate, the changes apply to distribution periods beginning on or after 6 April 1999 or distribution periods for which the distribution date is after 5 April 1999.

Section 490 of the Taxes Act 1988

9 (1) Section 490 of the Taxes Act 1988 (companies carrying on a mutual business or not carrying on a business) shall be amended as follows.

(2) In subsection (1) (which contains a reference to foreign income dividends) the words "or out of foreign income dividends" shall cease to have effect.

(3) In subsection (4) (which contains a reference to foreign income dividends) the words "or foreign income dividends" shall cease to have effect.

(4) Subsection (5) (definition of "foreign income dividends") shall cease to have effect.

(5) This paragraph has effect in relation to distributions made on or after 6th April 1999.

MUTUAL COMPANIES ETC

This paragraph removes spent references to FIDs in TA 1988 s 490 as regards post-5 April 1999 distributions.

Section 687 of the Taxes Act 1988

10 (1) In section 687 of the Taxes Act 1988 (payments under discretionary trusts) in subsection (3), paragraph (aaa) (which concerns any sums treated under section 246D(4) as income of trustees) shall cease to have effect.

(2) This paragraph has effect in relation to distributions made on or after 6th April 1999.

DISCRETIONARY TRUSTS, TRUST EXPENSES AND ESTATES IN ADMINISTRATION

TA 1988 s 687 provides for tax at the rate applicable to trusts to be assessable on trustees of certain trusts where they make distributions (treated as gross sums from which such tax has been withheld) to beneficiaries. Section 687(3) provides for certain amounts to be set off against tax otherwise assessable on the trustees including tax in respect of FIDs. This paragraph removes the reference to FIDs (in s 687(3)(*aaa*)) in respect of post-5 April 1999 distributions.

Section 689B of the Taxes Act 1988

11 (1) In section 689B of the Taxes Act 1988 (order in which expenses to be set against income) in subsection (2)(*b*) the words ''246D(4) or'' shall cease to have effect.

(2) This paragraph has effect in relation to distributions made on or after 6th April 1999.

GENERAL NOTE

This paragraph makes similar consequential amendments to para 10 above to TA 1988 s 689B, s 699 and s 701.

Section 699A of the Taxes Act 1988

12 (1) In section 699A of the Taxes Act 1988 (untaxed sums comprised in the income of the estate)—

  (*a*) in subsection (1)(*a*), and
  (*b*) in subsection (4)(*a*),

the word ''246D(3)'' shall cease to have effect.

(2) This paragraph has effect in relation to distributions made on or after 6th April 1999.

GENERAL NOTE

This paragraph makes similar consequential amendments to para 10 above to TA 1988 s 689B, s 699 and s 701.

Section 701 of the Taxes Act 1988

13 (1) In section 701 of the Taxes Act 1988 (interpretation) in subsection (8) (subjection for section 246D(3) etc) the word ''246D(3)'' shall cease to have effect.

(2) This paragraph has effect in relation to distributions made on or after 6th April 1999.

GENERAL NOTE

This paragraph makes similar consequential amendments to para 10 above to TA 1988 s 689B, s 699 and s 701.

Section 731 of the Taxes Act 1988

14 (1) Section 731 of the Taxes Act 1988 (application and interpretation of sections 732 to 734) shall be amended as follows.

(2) In subsection (9A) (application of references to interest in relation to a qualifying distribution other than a foreign income dividend) the words "other than a foreign income dividend" shall cease to have effect.

(3) Subsections (9B) to (9D) (which make provision in relation to foreign income dividends) shall cease to have effect.

(4) This paragraph has effect in relation to distributions made on or after 6th April 1999.

REPOS

TA 1988 ss 732–734 are anti-avoidance provisions dealing with, inter alia, sales of interest and dividend producing investments to enable the purchaser to receive income and then their repurchase ex div. Consequent upon the abolition of FIDs, spent references to FIDs in s 731(9A) and sub-s (9B) in their entirety, are removed by para 14 in respect of post-5 April 1999 distributions.

Section 802 of the Taxes Act 1988

15 (1) Section 802 of the Taxes Act 1988 (UK insurance companies trading overseas) shall be amended as follows.

(2) In subsection (2) (which contains a reference to foreign income dividends) the words "foreign income dividends" shall cease to have effect.

(3) Subsection (4) (definition of "foreign income dividends") shall cease to have effect.

(4) This paragraph has effect in relation to distributions made on or after 6th April 1999.

DOUBLE TAX RELIEF: INSURANCE COMPANIES

Restrictions on DTR for UK resident trading companies trading overseas referable to FIDs in TA 1988 s 802 are removed by para 15 consequent upon their abolition as regards post-5 April 1999 distributions.

Schedule 13 to the Taxes Act 1988

16 (1) Schedule 13 to the Taxes Act 1988 shall be amended as follows.

(2) In paragraph 1 (duty to make returns), in sub-paragraph (1)—

(*a*) paragraph (*b*) (duty to make returns of foreign income dividends paid and received) shall cease to have effect;

(b) in paragraph (c), the words "and foreign income dividends paid" shall cease to have effect; and

(c) the words following paragraph (c) (construction of references to foreign income dividends) shall cease to have effect.

(3) In sub-paragraph (4) of that paragraph—

(a) the word "4A(2),", and

(b) paragraph (b) and the word "and" immediately preceding it,

shall cease to have effect.

(4) In paragraph 2 (content of returns)—

(a) in sub-paragraph (1)—

(i) for "paragraphs 7(2), 3A(2) and 9A(2)" there shall be substituted "paragraph 7(2)"; and

(ii) paragraphs (d) to (f) (which require the return to include information in relation to foreign income dividends) shall cease to have effect; and

(b) sub-paragraphs (5) and (6) (which supplement paragraphs (e) and (f) of sub-paragraph (1)) shall cease to have effect.

(5) In paragraph 3 (payment of tax)—

(a) in sub-paragraph (1), the words "and foreign income dividends", and

(b) in sub-paragraph (3), the words "or foreign income dividend",

shall cease to have effect.

(6) Paragraphs 3A and 3B (which make provision in relation to international headquarters companies paying foreign income dividends) shall cease to have effect.

(7) In paragraph 4 (receipt of franked investment income after payment of advance corporation tax) in sub-paragraph (2) the words "or paid any foreign income dividends" shall cease to have effect.

(8) Paragraph 4A (receipt of foreign income dividends after payment of advance corporation tax) shall cease to have effect.

(9) Paragraph 6A (claims for set-off in respect of foreign income dividends received by a company) shall cease to have effect.

(10) In paragraph 7 (qualifying distributions which are not payments and payments of uncertain nature) in sub-paragraph (3) the words "and no foreign income dividend is paid" shall cease to have effect.

(11) Paragraph 9A (manufactured foreign income dividends) shall cease to have effect.

(12) Sub-paragraph (2) above has effect for accounting periods beginning on or after 6th April 1999.

(13) Sub-paragraphs (3) to (10) above have effect for return periods beginning on or after 6th April 1999.

(14) Sub-paragraph (11) above has effect in relation to manufactured dividends which are representative of dividends paid on or after 6th April 1999.

TA 1988 SCH 13: ACCOUNTING FOR ACT/INFORMATION PROVISION IN RESPECT OF FIDS

This paragraph removes unnecessary references to FIDs in Sch 13 for APs or return periods, as the case may be, beginning after 5 April 1999 and manufactured dividends representative of dividends paid after 5 April 1999.

Schedule 23A to the Taxes Act 1988

17 (1) Schedule 23A to the Taxes Act 1988 (manufactured dividends and interest) shall be amended as follows.

(2) In paragraph 1(1) (interpretation) the definition of "foreign income dividend" shall cease to have effect.

(3) In paragraph 2 (manufactured dividends on UK equities: general) in sub-paragraph (6) the words "Subject to paragraph 2B(2)(*b*) below" shall cease to have effect.

(4) Paragraph 2B (manufactured dividends representative of foreign income dividends) shall cease to have effect.

(5) This paragraph has effect in relation to manufactured dividends which are representative of dividends paid on or after 6th April 1999.

MANUFACTURED DIVIDENDS

This paragraph removes unnecessary references to FIDs in, and para 2B of, TA 1988 Sch 23A as regards manufactured dividends representative of post-5 April 1999 dividends (which could not be FIDs as a result of the abolition of FIDs).

Section 88A of the Finance Act 1989

18 (1) In section 88A of the Finance Act 1989 (lower corporation tax rate on certain insurance company profits) in subsection (3)—

(*a*) paragraph (*d*)(ii) (which relates to foreign income distributions) shall cease to have effect; and

(*b*) the words "(or by that subsection as applied by section 468R(2) of that Act)" shall cease to have effect.

(2) This paragraph has effect in relation to distributions made on or after 6th April 1999.

INSURANCE COMPANIES; FURTHER

This paragraph removes appropriate references to FIDs and distributions to corporate holders of units in AUTs in, respectively, FA 1989 ss 88A and 89 as regards post-5 April 1999 distributions.

Section 89 of the Finance Act 1989

19 (1) Section 89 of the Finance Act 1989 (policy holders' share of profits) shall be amended as follows.

(2) In subsection (2), paragraph (*c*) (which provides for Case I profits to be

reduced by the shareholders' share of any foreign income dividends from investments held in connection with life assurance business) shall cease to have effect.

(3) Subsection (2A) (which explains certain expressions used in subsection (2)(*c*)) shall cease to have effect.

(4) This paragraph has effect in relation to distributions made on or after 6th April 1999.

INSURANCE COMPANIES; FURTHER

This paragraph removes appropriate references to FIDs and distributions to corporate holders of units in AUTs in, respectively, FA 1989 ss 88A and 89 as regards post-5 April 1999 distributions.

Section 171 of the Finance Act 1993

20 (1) Section 171 of the Finance Act 1993 (taxation of profits and allowance of losses of Lloyd's underwriters) shall be amended as follows.

(2) Subsection (2A) (which makes provision in relation to foreign income dividends) shall cease to have effect.

(3) This paragraph has effect in relation to distributions made on or after 6th April 1999.

LLOYDS UNDERWRITERS

This paragraph removes spent references to FIDs in FA 1993 s 171 for post-5 April 1999 distributions.

Schedule 7 to the Finance Act 1997

21 (1) Schedule 7 to the Finance Act 1997 shall be amended as follows.

(2) Paragraph 2 (distributions treated as FIDs) shall cease to have effect.

(3) Paragraphs 4 to 6 (exceptions for stock options, dividends on fixed rate preference shares and pre-sale distributions) shall cease to have effect.

(4) Sub-paragraphs (2) and (3) above have effect in relation to distributions made on or after 6th April 1999.

DEEMED FIDS

This paragraph removes the operative parts of FA 1997 Sch 7 (deemed FIDs) as regards post-5 April 1999 distributions.

Transitional provisions

22 (1) Where, in the case of an accounting period of a company beginning before 6th April 1999 and ending on or after 5th April 1999 ("a transitional period"), there would (apart from this sub-paragraph) be such an excess as is mentioned in section 246F(3) of the Taxes Act 1988, no such excess shall be deemed to have arisen.

(2) In their application in relation to foreign income dividends paid in an accounting period of a company beginning before 6th April 1999, sections 246J(5) and 246K(10) of the Taxes Act 1988 shall have effect as if the reference to any subsequent accounting period—

(*a*) included an accounting period which immediately follows a transitional period, but

(*b*) did not include any later accounting period.

TRANSITIONAL PROVISIONS

Sub-paragraph (1) provides that any excess of FIDs received over FIDs paid in an accounting period commencing before 6 April 1999 but ending on or after 5 April 1999 (a "transitional period") cannot be carried forward to later periods as otherwise provided by TA 1988 s 246F(3).

Sub-paragraph (2) makes it clear that where a company has paid an FID in an AP commencing before 6 April 1999 it may match the FID against a distributable foreign profit of a transitional period or an AP immediately following the transitional period, whether of the paying company in accordance with s 246J(5) or an eligible subsidiary in accordance with s 246K(10), but not subsequent APs.

23 Where a foreign income dividend paid by a company before 6th April 1999—

(*a*) is received by a person on or after that date, and

(*b*) is not one in relation to which section 246D of the Taxes Act 1988 applies,

the recipient shall be treated, for all purposes of the Tax Acts, as receiving instead a qualifying distribution made by a company resident in the United Kingdom of an amount equal to nine tenths of the amount of the foreign income dividend.

BACKGROUND NOTE

This paragraph deals with the position of FIDs paid before 6 April 1999 but received on or after that date by corporate recipients (individuals, PRs and trustees are generally persons to which TA 1988 s 246D applies, and therefore by para 23(*b*) excluded). The recipients are treated as receiving a conventional qualifying distribution of 9/10ths of the actual amount of the FID.

SCHEDULE 7

RESTRICTIONS ON GROUP RELIEF

BACKGROUND NOTE

Group relief and consortium group relief apply to enable the tax losses (including trading losses, charges on income, expenses of management, foreign exchange losses, losses on transactions in financial instruments and loan relationship deficits) of a loss-making group member to be surrendered to and offset against the taxable total profits of other group members. This system of relief has been in place, though amended from time to time, since well before the introduction of corporation tax in the UK in 1965.

For these purposes, members of a group of companies are all UK resident companies which have a common equity relationship of at least 75 per cent (that is, either a common parent, resident in the UK, owns at least 75 per cent of the equity in the claimant and surrendering companies or one of the companies owns at least 75 per cent of the equity in the other). A consortium company is a UK resident company which is at least 75 per cent owned by a number of companies, none of whom own less than 5 per cent of the equity, nor may the consortium company be a 75 per cent subsidiary of any company, other than a holding company which is itself owned by a consortium.

A key feature of the UK system of group relief, unlike that of a number of other countries, is that it is available between companies which do not have identical accounting periods. The previous legislation required "corresponding accounting periods" (ie parts of corporation tax accounting periods which were common to both the surrendering and claimant companies, and during which they both met the criteria for group membership) to be identified and the profits and losses which were potentially available for group relief to be apportioned where necessary.

Apportionment remains on a time basis except where only an alternative method of computing the figure would produce a just and reasonable result. However, prior to 2 July 1997, the apportionment basis arriving at the corresponding accounting period's profit or loss did not look at the cumulative result. In cases where the members of a group had accounting periods of different lengths or ending on different dates, it did not prevent successive group relief claims by more than one company from utilising more loss than would strictly have been available on a cumulative basis. This could, on occasion, result in 12 months' losses being surrendered by way of group relief to several claimant companies where there was, perhaps, only a six months' corresponding period.

The amendments in Sch 7, which apply from 2 July 1997, seek to correct this defect in the legislation. Paragraph 2 introduces new TA 1988 ss 403A, 403B and 403C. Paragraphs 3–5 provide consequential amendments to ss 403(9) (deleting the rules for computing the fraction limiting relief in consortium claims), 405(4) (consequent on removal of s 403(9)) and in s 406 (removing references to s 403(9) and inserting references to the new sections). Paragraphs 7 and 8 amend TA 1988 s 413 (clarification on the meaning of common accounting periods) and TCGA 1992 s 179 (inserting references to the new sections) respectively, while para 6 deletes ss 408 (corresponding accounting periods), 409 (companies joining or leaving the group or consortium) and sub-ss 411(2)–411(9) (exclusion of double allowances). Finally, para 9 provides commencement and transitional rules.

NEW TA 1988 S 403A

The concept of the corresponding period is replaced by new rules dealing with an "overlapping period".

SUBSECTIONS (1)–12(3)

The maximum loss to be surrendered is to be the smaller of the unused part of the total available or the unrelieved part of the total profit of the claimant company in the overlapping period.

The unused part of the loss is the part remaining after prior surrenders of loss. This assumes that the total loss available for the overlapping period is computed and successive surrenders of loss are deducted from that total until the whole of the loss for the overlapping period is exhausted.

The unrelieved part of the total profit assumes an apportionment of the total profit for the entire accounting period between the amount for the overlapping period and the balance. The profit for the overlapping period is then taken and successive group relief claims are deducted from it until, cumulatively, the profit is exhausted.

EXAMPLE

Company A

Accounting period to 31 December 1998—Loss	£160,000
Overlapping periods	
1 April 1998 to 30 June 1998 (3/12)	£40,000
1 July 1998 to 31 December 1998 (6/12)	£80,000
Non-overlapping period	
1 January 1998 to 31 March 1998	£40,000

Company B

Accounting period to 31 July 1999—Profit	£100,000
Overlapping period	
1 July 1998 to 31 December 1998 (6/12)	£50,000

Company C

Accounting period to 31 March 1999—Profit	£120,000
Overlapping period	
1 April 1998 to 31 December 1998 (9/12)	£90,000

Group relief allocations
Surrenders by Company A

	Period to 30.6.98	Period to 31.12.98	Total
Available loss	£40,000	£80,000	£120,000
Surrendered to Company C	(30,000)	(60,000)	(90,000)
Surrendered to Company A		(20,000)	(20,000)
Unused part of loss	10,000		10,000

SUBSECTIONS (4) AND (5)

A strict hierarchy of prior claims and surrenders is imposed. Each relevant claim is aggregated to all the prior claims (which have not, at that point, been withdrawn) and deducted from the total amount of the surrenderable loss. After each cumulative calculation the balance of unused loss is struck. A similar process applies to the potentially group relievable profits of a claimant company.

SUBSECTIONS (6) AND (7)

In future considerable care will need to be taken in prioritising the sequence of group relief surrenders and claims.

A claim is finalised at the time when, under the legislation contained in TA 1988 Sch 17A, it may no longer be withdrawn and finalised claims have priority over claims which, though made, can still be withdrawn (ie, where the time limit for making the election has not yet expired). Where there is more than one claim made by a company and it happens that the time limit expires earlier for one or the other claim (precluding any subsequent withdrawal), the earlier claim is treated as having priority (since it was finalised first).

However, this automatic prioritisation may be over-ridden. Companies jointly making elections to respectively surrender and claim group relief will be able to specify the order in which losses are to be allocated to claimant companies. Power is also given to the Board of Inland Revenue to direct the order of claims in the absence of a formal election.

SUBSECTIONS (8)–(10)

The "overlapping period" is the period throughout which both the claimant and the surrendering companies have met the qualifying conditions for group relief (as to membership of the group or consortium) and which is a common period within the corporation tax accounting periods of both companies.

NEW TA 1988 S 403B

The formula approach of TA 1988 s 408 (which ceases to have effect for periods from 2 July 1997) has been replaced by a simpler formulation. Except where the accounting period of the claimant and the surrendering companies correspond exactly, an apportionment is required. Generally it will be on a time basis to arrive at figures for the common period, but where a time basis of apportionment would not produce a just and reasonable result, an alternative method, which does produce it, must be substituted.

The alternative method will usually be based on figures derived from internal management accounts, which produce the actual figures of profit earned or loss in the common period. However, the reluctance of the legislators to open this door is evident in the addition of the qualification, in TA 1988 s 403B(2), "to the extent only that is necessary". Even where internal accounting figures are more accurate than time-apportioned figures, they may not be used unless there is a manifest injustice in using the time-apportioned figures.

NEW TA 1988 S 403C

The existing rules for apportionment of consortium relief claims have been removed from TA 1988 s 403(9) and largely incorporated in this new section. Effectively, this ensures that the relief claimed can be no more than the consortium member's proportionate share in the equity of the consortium subsidiary. In addition, the cumulation rules of new TA 1988 s 403A are also adapted for the purposes of consortium relief.

COMMENCEMENT AND TRANSITIONAL RULES

The new provisions apply where an accounting period of either a surrendering or a claimant company ends after 2 July 1997.

Where an accounting period spans 2 July 1997, the relief available is to be computed on two bases. First, a calculation is required on the basis that the new provisions had not been enacted. Second, taking a commencement date of 2 July for the calculation, the loss or profit available for group relief is computed under the new provisions. This latter calculation is then compared to what the relief would have been if the new provisions had not been enacted and an amount equal to the relief that has been withdrawn is deducted from the first calculation.

In effect this means that all calculations of group relief in respect of an accounting period of a company spanning 2 July 1997 require to be done on the basis that there are two notional accounting periods. The period prior to 3 July is subject to the old rules, while the period from 2 July is subject to the new rules.

Introductory

1 Chapter IV of Part X of the Taxes Act 1988 (group relief) shall be amended in accordance with paragraphs 2 to 7 below.

New limits

2 The following sections shall be inserted after section 403—

"403A Limits on group relief

(1) The amount which, on a claim for group relief, may be set off against the total profits of the claimant company for an accounting period ("the claim period"), and accordingly the amount to which any consent required in respect of that claim may relate, shall not exceed whichever is the smaller of the following amounts—

(*a*) the unused part of the surrenderable amount for the overlapping period; and

(*b*) the unrelieved part of the claimant company's total profits for the overlapping period.

(2) For the purposes of any claim for group relief—

(*a*) the unused part of the surrenderable amount for the overlapping period is the surrenderable amount for that period reduced by the amount of any prior surrenders attributable to the overlapping period; and

(*b*) the unrelieved part of the claimant company's total profits for the overlapping period is the amount of its total profits for that period reduced by the amount of any previously claimed group relief attributable to the overlapping period.

(3) For the purposes of any claim for group relief—

(*a*) the surrenderable amount for the overlapping period is so much of the surrenderable amount for the accounting period of the surrendering company to which the claim relates as is attributable, on an apportionment in accordance with section 403B, to the overlapping period;

(*b*) the surrenderable amount for an accounting period of the surrendering company is the total amount for that accounting period of the losses and other amounts which (disregarding this section and section 403C) are available in that company's case for set off by way of group relief; and

(*c*) the amount of the claimant company's total profits for the overlapping period is so much of its total profits for the claim period as is attributable, on an apportionment in accordance with section 403B, to the overlapping period.

(4) In relation to any claim for group relief ("the relevant claim") the amount of the prior surrenders attributable to the period which is the

overlapping period in the case of the relevant claim is equal to the aggregate amount (if any) produced by—

(*a*) taking the amount of every claim for group relief (whether a group claim or a consortium claim) which—

(i) has been made before the relevant claim,

(ii) was made in respect of the whole or any part of the amount which, in relation to the relevant claim, is the surrenderable amount for the accounting period of the surrendering company to which the claim relates, and

(iii) has not been withdrawn;

(*b*) treating the amount of group relief which (having regard to the provisions of this section) is allowable under each such claim as an amount of relief for the period which is the overlapping period in the case of that claim;

(*c*) determining how much of each amount treated in accordance with paragraph (*b*) above as an amount of relief for a particular period is attributable, on an apportionment in accordance with section 403B, to the period (if any) which is common to both—

(i) that period; and

(ii) the period which is the overlapping period in the case of the relevant claim;

and

(*d*) aggregating all the amounts determined under paragraph (*c*) above in respect of the previously made claims.

(5) In relation to any claim for group relief ("the relevant claim"), the amount of previously claimed group relief attributable to the period which is the overlapping period in the case of that claim is the aggregate amount produced by—

(*a*) taking the amount of every claim for group relief (whether a group claim or a consortium claim) which—

(i) has been made before the relevant claim,

(ii) was a claim to set off an amount by way of group relief against the claimant company's total profits for the period which, in relation to the relevant claim, is the claim period, and

(iii) has not been withdrawn;

(*b*) treating the amount of group relief which (having regard to the provisions of this section) is allowable under each such claim as an amount of relief for the period which is the overlapping period in the case of that claim;

(*c*) determining how much of each amount treated in accordance with paragraph (*b*) above as an amount of relief for a particular period is attributable, on an apportionment in accordance with section 403B, to the period (if any) which is common to both—

(i) that period; and

(ii) the period which is the overlapping period in the case of the relevant claim;

and

(*d*) aggregating all the amounts determined under paragraph (*c*) above in respect of the previously made claims.

(6) For the purposes of this section the amount of group relief allowable on any claim ("the finalised claim") shall fall to be determined as at the time when that claim ceases to be capable of being withdrawn as if—

(*a*) every claim that became incapable of being withdrawn before that time were a claim made before the finalised claim; and

(*b*) every claim that remains capable of being withdrawn at that time were a claim made after the finalised claim.

(7) Subject to subsection (6) above and without prejudice to any power to withdraw and resubmit claims, where (but for this subsection) more than one claim for group relief would be taken for the purposes of subsections (4) and (5) above to have been made at the same time, those claims shall be deemed, instead, to have been made—

(*a*) in such order as the company or companies making them may, by notice to any officer of the Board, elect or, as the case may be, jointly elect; and

(*b*) if there is no such election, in such order as an officer of the Board may direct.

(8) In this section "the overlapping period", in relation to a claim for group relief, means (subject to subsection (9) below and section 406(3) and (7)) the period which is common to both—

(*a*) the claim period; and

(*b*) the accounting period of the surrendering company to which the claim relates.

(9) For the purposes of this section any time in the period which, in relation to any claim for group relief, is common to both the accounting periods mentioned in subsection (8) above but which is a time when the qualifying conditions were not satisfied—

(*a*) shall be treated as not comprised in the period which is the overlapping period in the case of that claim; and

(*b*) shall be treated instead, in relation to each of those accounting periods, as if it constituted a part of that accounting period which was not common to both periods.

(10) For the purposes of subsection (9) above the qualifying conditions are satisfied in relation to any claim for group relief at the following times, that is to say—

(*a*) if the claim is a group claim, whenever the claimant company and the surrendering company are both members of the same group; and

(*b*) if the claim is a consortium claim, whenever the conditions specified in section 402(3) for the making of that claim are satisfied in the case of the claimant company and the surrendering company.

403B Apportionments under section 403A

(1) Subject to subsection (2) below, where an apportionment falls to be

made under section 403A for the purpose of determining how much of an amount for any period ("the first period") is attributable to any other period ("the second period") which comprises the whole or a part of the first period—

(*a*) the whole of that amount shall be attributed to the second period if the first and second periods begin and end at the same times; and

(*b*) in any other case, the apportionment shall be made on a time basis according to how much of the first period coincides with the second period.

(2) Where the circumstances of a particular case are such that the making on the time basis mentioned in subsection (1)(*b*) above of some or all of the apportionments to be made in that case would work in a manner that would be unjust or unreasonable in relation to any person, those apportionments shall be made instead (to the extent only that is necessary in order to avoid injustice and unreasonableness) in such other manner as may be just and reasonable.

403C   Special rules for consortium cases

(1) Where—

(*a*) in the case of a consortium claim, the surrendering company is a member of the consortium, and

(*b*) the amount produced by multiplying the surrenderable amount for the overlapping period by the relevant fraction is less than the smaller of the amounts given by subsection (1)(*a*) and (*b*) of section 403A,

the amount which, on that claim, may be set off against the total profits of the claimant company for the claim period shall not exceed the amount produced by that multiplication.

(2) Where—

(*a*) in the case of a consortium claim, the claimant company is a member of the consortium, and

(*b*) the amount produced by multiplying the claimant company's total profits for the overlapping period by the relevant fraction is less than the smaller of the amounts given by subsection (1)(*a*) and (*b*) of section 403A,

the amount which, on that claim, may be set off against the total profits of the claimant company for the claim period shall not exceed the amount produced by that multiplication.

(3) For the purposes of this section the relevant fraction is the fraction equivalent to—

(*a*) in a case falling within subsection (1) above, the surrendering company's member's share in the consortium in the accounting period of that company which is or includes the overlapping period; and

(*b*) in a case falling within subsection (2) above, the claimant company's member's share in the consortium in the accounting period of that company which is or includes the overlapping period.

(4) Expressions used in this section and in section 403A have the same meanings in this section as in that section.''

Consequential amendments

3 Subsection (9) of section 403 (fraction limiting relief in the case of consortium claims) shall cease to have effect.

4 In section 405(4) (claims relating to losses of members of both groups and consortia), for the words from "a fraction" to "403(9)(*b*))" there shall be substituted "which an amount may by virtue of that claim be set off by way of group relief".

5 (1) In section 406 (consortium claims by or in relation to group members and consortium companies), in each of subsections (2) and (6) (which refer to the fraction in section 403(9))—

(*a*) for "appropriate under section 403(9)" there shall be substituted "the relevant fraction for the purposes of section 403C"; and
(*b*) for "that which would be appropriate" there shall be substituted "it would be".

(2) For subsection (3) of that section there shall be substituted the following subsection—

"(3) Sections 403A to 403C shall have effect in relation to a consortium claim made by a group member by virtue of subsection (2) above as if any time when the claimant company was not a member of the group—

(*a*) were not comprised in the period which is the overlapping period in the case of that claim; and
(*b*) were to be treated instead as if it constituted a part of the claim period which did not coincide with any part of the accounting period of the surrendering company to which the claim relates."

(3) For subsection (7) of that section there shall be substituted the following subsection—

"(7) Sections 403A to 403C shall have effect in relation to a consortium claim made by a consortium company by virtue of subsection (5) above as if any time when the surrendering company was not a member of the group—

(*a*) were not comprised in the period which is the overlapping period in the case of that claim; and
(*b*) were to be treated instead as if it constituted a part of the claim period that did not coincide with any part of the accounting period of the surrendering company to which the claim relates."

(4) In subsection (8) of that section, for the words from "that fraction" to "409(3)(*b*)" there shall be substituted "the maximum amount of relief available to the claimant company".

6 Sections 408, 409 and 411(2) to (9) (which limit group relief where the accounting periods of the claimant company and the surrendering company do not coincide and where companies join and leave groups and make other provision for excluding double relief) shall cease to have effect.

7 In section 413 (interpretation), after subsection (2) there shall be inserted the following subsection—

"(2A) For the purposes of group relief an accounting period of the claimant company which falls wholly or partly within an accounting period of the surrendering company shall be taken to correspond to that accounting period of the surrendering company."

8 In section 179(4) of the Taxation of Chargeable Gains Act 1992 (which specifies when a gain or loss on de-grouping is deemed to accrue), for the words after paragraph (*b*) there shall be substituted—

"and sections 403A and 403B of the Taxes Act (limits on group relief) shall have effect accordingly as if the actual circumstances were as they are treated as having been."

Commencement

9 (1) This Schedule has effect, subject to sub-paragraphs (2) to (4) below, in relation to any claim for group relief if—

(*a*) the accounting period of the claimant company for which relief is claimed, or

(*b*) the accounting period of the surrendering company to which that claim relates,

is an accounting period ending on or after 2nd July 1997.

(2) This Schedule does not apply in relation to any claim for group relief for which the overlapping period for the purposes of section 403A of the Taxes Act 1988 would be a period falling entirely before 2nd July 1997.

(3) Where in the case of any claim for group relief the overlapping period begins before but ends on or after 2nd July 1997, the maximum amount which in the claimant's case is allowable on that claim by way of group relief shall (instead of being determined in accordance with this Schedule) be the amount determined by—

(*a*) taking the maximum amount that would have been allowable on that claim if this Schedule had not been enacted; and

(*b*) reducing that amount by the amount (if any) of the relief withdrawn in respect of the part of the claimant company's accounting period beginning with 2nd July 1997.

(4) For the purposes of sub-paragraph (3) above the relief withdrawn in respect of the part of the claimant company's accounting period beginning with 2nd July 1997 is the amount (if any) by which the amount specified in paragraph (*a*) below exceeds the amount specified in paragraph (*b*) below, that is to say—

(*a*) the maximum amount which would have been allowable by way of group relief on the claimant company's claim if this Schedule had not been enacted but it were assumed that the qualifying conditions were not satisfied in relation to that claim at any time before 2nd July 1997; and

(*b*) the maximum amount which would be allowable by way of group relief on that claim if that were assumed but relief fell to be given in accordance with Chapter IV of Part X of the Taxes Act 1988 as amended by this Schedule.

(5) For the purposes of sub-paragraph (4) above an assumption in relation to any claim that the qualifying conditions were not satisfied at a particular time

is an assumption that, at that time, the claimant company and the surrendering company—

(*a*) were not both members of the same group; and

(*b*) did not satisfy in relation to each other the conditions specified in section 402(3) of the Taxes Act 1988 for the making of a consortium claim.

Section 52

SCHEDULE 8

REPEALS

PART I

VEHICLE LICENSING: PAYMENTS WHERE INFORMATION TO BE
TRANSMITTED ELECTRONICALLY

Chapter	Short title	Extent of repeal
1994 c 22	The Vehicle Excise and Registration Act 1994	Section 22(3).

PART II

INCOME TAX AND CORPORATION TAX

(1) RELIEF FOR MORTGAGE INTEREST PAYMENTS

Chapter	Short title	Extent of repeal
1988 c 1	The Income and Corporation Taxes Act 1988	In section 353(1G), the words after paragraph (*b*). In section 369(1A), the words after paragraph (*b*).

These repeals have effect in accordance with section 15 of this Act.

(2) MEDICAL INSURANCE RELIEF

Chapter	Short title	Extent of repeal
1989 c 26	The Finance Act 1989	Sections 54 to 57.
1994 c 9	The Finance Act 1994	Section 83. Schedule 10.
1996 c 8	The Finance Act 1996	In section 129— (*a*) paragraph (*a*) of subsection (1); (*b*) in subsection (2), the words "section 54(6)(*b*) of the 1989 Act and"; and (*c*) subsections (3) and (5). In Schedule 18— (*a*) paragraph 12; and

Chapter	Short title	Extent of repeal
1996 c 8— (contd)	The Finance Act 1996— (contd)	(*b*) in paragraph 17, the words "12(2)(*a*) and (*b*)" and "12(2)(*c*) and (3)" wherever occurring and the words "12(2)(*d*)" in sub-paragraph (8).

These repeals have effect for the year 1997–98 and subsequent years of assessment except in relation to the cases in which the relief that has been or may be given under section 54 of the Finance Act 1989 in respect of any payment is unaffected by the provisions of section 17(1) of this Act.

(3) CORPORATION TAX RATES

Chapter	Short title	Extent of repeal
1997 c 16	The Finance Act 1997	Section 58. Section 59(*a*).

(4) TAXATION OF DISTRIBUTIONS: SURPLUS FRANKED INVESTMENT INCOME

Chapter	Short title	Extent of repeal
1988 c 1	The Income and Corporation Taxes Act 1988	In section 6(4), the words "242, 243". In section 75(5), the words "or against a decision on a claim under section 242". Sections 242 to 244. In section 704, in paragraph A, sub-paragraph (*e*). Section 825(4)(*d*). Section 826(7B).
1990 c 1	The Capital Allowances Act 1990	In Schedule 1, paragraph 8(11).
1991 c 31	The Finance Act 1991	In Schedule 15, paragraphs 5 and 6.
1993 c 34	The Finance Act 1993	In section 78, subsections (8) to (10), and in subsection (11) the words from "but this subsection" to the end.

Chapter	Short title	Extent of repeal
1995 c 4	The Finance Act 1995	In Schedule 8, in paragraph 18, sub-paragraphs (7) and (8).
1996 c 8	The Finance Act 1996	In Schedule 14, paragraph 12.
1997 c 16	The Finance Act 1997	Section 71.

These repeals have effect in accordance with section 20 of this Act (and, accordingly, the repeal of subsection (7B) of section 826 of the Income and Corporation Taxes Act 1988 has effect only where the earlier period mentioned in that subsection begins on or after 2nd July 1997).

(5) LLOYD'S UNDERWRITERS

Chapter	Short title	Extent of repeal
1993 c 34	The Finance Act 1993	In paragraph 13 of Schedule 19— (*a*) in sub-paragraph (1), paragraph (*b*) and the word "or" immediately preceding it; (*b*) in sub-paragraph (3), the words "or paid" and, in sub-paragraph (*a*), the words "or (as the case may be) that part of that income which includes the qualifying distribution"; (*c*) sub-paragraphs (3A); and (*d*) sub-paragraph (4A).
1994 c 9	The Finance Act 1994	In section 219(4), the words "(and any associated tax credits)". In section 221(2), paragraph (*b*), and paragraph (*d*) and the word "and" immediately preceding it. In Schedule 21, paragraph 11.

These repeals have effect in relation to distributions made on or after 2nd July 1997.

(6) INSURANCE COMPANIES AND FRIENDLY SOCIETIES: REPEALS
OTHER THAN THOSE RELATING TO SELF-ASSESSMENT

Chapter	Short title	Extent of repeal
1988 c 1	The Income and Corporation Taxes Act 1988	In section 76(8), the definition of "relevant franked investment income". In section 432E(6), paragraph (*b*) and the word "and" immediately preceding it. In section 434, in subsection (3), the words from "but it may be the subject of a claim" onwards, and, in subsection (8), the words from "or by payment of tax credit" onwards. Section 434A(1). In section 436(3), paragraphs (*d*) and (*e*). In section 438, subsections (3), (3AA), (5) to (7) and (9). Section 439B(7). Section 440B(1A) and (2). Section 441A(1). In paragraph 1 of Schedule 19AB— (*a*) in sub-paragraph (1), the words "the aggregate of", and paragraph (*b*) and the word "and" immediately preceding it; (*b*) in sub-paragraph (7), the words "paid or", paragraph (*b*) and the word "and" immediately preceding it, and the words "or in section 42(5A) of the Management Act"; (*c*) sub-paragraph (8); and

Chapter	Short title	Extent of repeal
1988 c 1— (contd)	The Income and Corporation Taxes Act 1988—(contd)	(*d*) in sub-paragraph (10), the words "and payments of tax credits" and "or in section 42(5A) of the Management Act". In Schedule 19AC, paragraph 2, in paragraph 5(1), the notionally inserted section 76(6B), in paragraph 5B, sub-paragraphs (1) to (3), and paragraphs 9A, 10, 10A, 11A(1), 12(1) and 15(1).
1989 c 26	The Finance Act 1989	In section 89, in subsection (2), paragraph (*a*) and, in paragraph (*b*), the words "other unrelieved", and subsection (8).
1990 c 29	The Finance Act 1990	Section 45(9). In Schedule 6, paragraph 5.
1994 c 9	The Finance Act 1994	In Schedule 16, paragraph 6.
1995 c 4	The Finance Act 1995	In Schedule 8, paragraphs 19(2), 28(2), 29, 35(2), 36, 41, 43 and 47.
1996 c 8	The Finance Act 1996	Section 164(2)(*b*) and (3)(*a*). In Schedule 14, paragraph 51. In Schedule 27, paragraph 5. In Schedule 34, paragraphs 1(7) and 5(2).

Except for the repeals in Schedule 34 to the Finance Act 1996, these repeals have effect in accordance with the provisions of Schedule 3 to this Act, other than paragraph 11.

(7) INSURANCE COMPANIES AND FRIENDLY SOCIETIES: REPEALS
RELATING TO SELF-ASSESSMENT

Chapter	Short title	Extent of repeal
1988 c 1	The Income and Corporation Taxes Act 1988	In paragraph 1 of Schedule 19AB, in sub-paragraph (7), the words "paid or", paragraph (*b*) and the word "and" immediately preceding it, and the words "or section 42(4) of the Management Act". In paragraph 3 of Schedule 19AB— (*a*) in sub-paragraph (1A), the words "paid or" and "or section 42(4) of the Management Act", and paragraph (*b*) and the word "and" immediately preceding it; (*b*) in sub-paragraph (1B), the words "payments or" and paragraph (*b*) and the word "or" immediately preceding it; and (*c*) in sub-paragraph (8), the words "paid or" and paragraph (*b*) and the word "or" immediately preceding it.

These repeals have effect in accordance with paragraphs 11 and 12 of Schedule 3 to this Act.

(8) TAXATION OF DEALERS IN RESPECT OF DISTRIBUTIONS ETC

Chapter	Short title	Extent of repeal
1988 c 1	The Income and Corporation Taxes Act 1988	In section 95, in subsection (1A), paragraphs (*b*) and (*d*), subsection (1B), in subsection (2), the word "qualifying" in both places where it occurs, and subsections (4) and (5).

Chapter	Short title	Extent of repeal
1988 c 1— (contd)	The Income and Corporation Taxes Act 1988—(contd)	In section 234(1), the words "but subject to section 95(1A)(*c*)". In section 732 subsections (2) and (2A), in subsection (4) the words "on a stock exchange outside the United Kingdom", and subsections (5) to (7). Section 738(1)(*a*) and (*b*). In Schedule 23A, paragraph 2A(2). In Schedule 28B, in paragraph 13(5), paragraph (*b*) and the word "and" immediately preceding it.
1990 c 29	The Finance Act 1990	Section 53(1).
1991 c 31	The Finance Act 1991	Section 56.
1997 c 16	The Finance Act 1997	In Schedule 7, paragraph 2(3)(*a*).

1 The repeals in sections 95 and 234 of, and Schedule 23A to, the Income and Corporation Taxes Act 1988 and in Schedule 7 to the Finance Act 1997 have effect in accordance with section 24 of this Act.

2 The repeals in sections 732 and 738 of the Income and Corporation Taxes Act 1988 and section 53 of the Finance Act 1990, and the repeal of section 56 of the Finance Act 1991, have effect in accordance with section 26 of this Act.

3 The repeal in Schedule 28B to the Income and Corporation Taxes Act 1988 has effect in accordance with section 25 of this Act.

(9) TAX CREDITS AND SCHEDULE F INCOME

Chapter	Short title	Extent of repeal
1970 c 9	The Taxes Management Act 1970	In section 42, subsections (4) and (4A) and in subsection (5), the words from "and the reference in subsection (4) above" onwards. In section 42, in subsection (5), the words "Subject to subsection (5A) below," and subsections (5A) and (10A).

Chapter	Short title	Extent of repeal
1988 c 1	The Income and Corporation Taxes Act 1988	In section 231, subsection (2), in subsection (3), the words from "and subject to" onwards and subsections (3A) to (3D). Section 231A. Section 232(2) and (3). Sections 235 to 237. In section 246(6)(*a*)(ii) the words "section 231(1) and". In section 709(2A), the words "and to a repayment of tax", "respectively" and "and to a payment of any amount in respect of a tax credit".
1989 c 26	The Finance Act 1989	Section 106.
1990 c 29	The Finance Act 1990	Section 97.
1993 c 34	The Finance Act 1993	In Schedule 6, paragraph 3.
1994 c 9	The Finance Act 1994	In Schedule 9, paragraph 2.
1995 c 4	The Finance Act 1995	Section 107(5) and (6).
1997 c 16	The Finance Act 1997	Section 70. In Schedule 7, paragraph 3.
1997 c 58	The Finance (No 2) Act 1997	Section 19.

1 The repeals in section 42 of the Taxes Management Act 1970 (and the related repeals of section 97 of the Finance Act 1990 and in section 107 of the Finance Act 1995) have effect in accordance with paragraphs 2 and 3 of Schedule 4 to this Act.

2 The repeal in section 709 of the Taxes Act 1988 has effect for the year of assessment 1999–00 and subsequent years of assessment.

3 The other repeals have effect in relation to distributions made on or after 6th April 1999.

(10) TAX CREDITS ETC: INSURANCE COMPANIES AND LLOYD'S UNDERWRITERS

Chapter	Short title	Extent of repeal
1988 c 1	The Income and Corporation Taxes Act 1988	In section 231B, in subsection (4)(*b*), the words "or 441 A(7)". In section 434(1A) the words from "but this subsection" onwards.

Chapter	Short title	Extent of repeal
1988 c 1— (contd)	The Income and Corporation Taxes Act 1988—(contd)	Section 441A(2) to (8). In Schedule 19AC, in paragraph 9(1), in the notionally inserted section 434(1D), the words from "but this subsection" onwards and paragraph 11A(2).
1993 c 34	The Finance Act 1993	In Schedule 20, paragraph 9(3) and, in paragraph 11(3)(*c*), the words "or tax credit received" and "or (3)".
1995 c 4	The Finance Act 1995	In Schedule 8, paragraph 31.

These repeals have effect in relation to distributions made on or after 6th April 1999.

(11) FOREIGN INCOME DIVIDENDS

Chapter	Short title	Extent of repeal
1988 c 1	The Income and Corporation Taxes Act 1988	In section 13, in subsection (7), the words "and with the addition of foreign income dividends arising to the company", and subsection (8A). In section 75, in subsection (2), the words "foreign income dividends", and subsection (6). Sections 246A to 246Y. Section 247(5A) to (5D). In section 431(2), the definition of "foreign income dividends". In section 434, subsections (3B) to (3D) and, in subsection (6A), paragraphs (*aa*) to (ac). In section 458(2), the words "and foreign income dividends arising to". Section 468H(5).

Chapter	Short title	Extent of repeal
1988 c 1— (contd)	The Income and Corporation Taxes Act 1988—(contd)	In section 468I, in subsection (2), the words "which are not foreign income dividends", and subsections (3), (5), (5A) and (7). In section 468J, in subsection (1), the words "or a part of the total amount" and "which are not foreign income dividends", in subsection (2), the words "or, as the case may be, the part", and subsection (3). Section 468K. Section 468M(5)(*c*). In section 468Q, in subsection (2)(*a*), the words "a foreign income distribution", in subsection (3), the definition of "B", and subsection (4). Section 468R. In section 490, in subsection (1), the words "or out of foreign income dividends", in subsection (4), the words "or foreign income dividends", and subsection (5). In section 687(3), paragraph (*aaa*). In section 689B(2)(*b*) the words "246D)(4) or". In section 699A, in subsections (1)(*a*) and (4)(*a*), the word "246D(3)". In section 701(8), the word "246D(3)". In section 731, in subsection (9A), the words "other than a foreign income dividend", and subsections (9B) to (9D).

Chapter	Short title	Extent of repeal
1988 c 1— (contd)	The Income and Corporation Taxes Act 1988—(contd)	In section 802, in subsection (2), the words "foreign income dividends", and subsection (4). In paragraph 1 of Schedule 13— (*a*) in sub-paragraph (1), paragraph (*b*), in paragraph (*c*) the words "and foreign income dividends paid", and the words following paragraph (*c*); (*b*) in sub-paragraph (4), the word "4A(2),", and paragraph (*b*) and the word "and" immediately preceding it. In paragraph 2 of Schedule 13, sub-paragraphs (1)(*d*) to (f) and (5) and (6). In paragraph 3 of Schedule 13, in sub-paragraph (1), the words "and foreign income dividends", and in sub-paragraph (3), the words "or foreign income dividend". In Schedule 13, paragraphs 3A and 3B. In paragraph 4(2) of Schedule 13, the words "or paid any foreign income dividends". In Schedule 13, paragraphs 4A and 6A. In paragraph 7(3) of Schedule 13, the words "and no foreign income dividend is paid". In Schedule 13, paragraph 9A. In Schedule 23A, in paragraph 1(1), the definition of "foreign

Chapter	Short title	Extent of repeal
1988 c 1— (contd)	The Income and Corporation Taxes Act 1988—(contd)	income dividend'', in paragraph 2(6), the words ''Subject to paragraph 2B(2)(*b*) below'', and paragraph 2B.
1989 c 26	The Finance Act 1989	In section 88A(3), paragraph (*d*)(ii) and the word ''or'' immediately preceding it, and the words ''(or by that subsection as applied by section 468R(2) of that Act)''. In section 89, in subsection (2), paragraph (*c*) and the word ''and'' immediately preceding it, and subsection (2A).
1993 c 34	The Finance Act 1993	Section 171(2A).
1994 c 9	The Finance Act 1994	In Schedule 16, paragraph 1, in paragraph 3, sub-paragraphs (5) to (10) and (12), and paragraphs 4, 5(4) and (5), 7 to 9 and 11 to 16. In Schedule 21, paragraph 1(1) and (3)(*a*).
1995 c 4	The Finance Act 1995	Section 76(1).
1996 c 8	The Finance Act 1996	Section 122(5)(*a*). In Schedule 6, paragraph 5. In Schedule 23, paragraphs 4 and 6. In Schedule 27, paragraphs 1 to 4 and 6. In Schedule 38, in paragraph 6, sub-paragraph (2)(*c*) and, in sub-paragraph (5), the words ''(2)(*c*) and''.
1997 c 16	The Finance Act 1997	Section 72. In Schedule 7, paragraphs 2, 4 to 6 and 9 to 11. In Schedule 10, paragraphs 9 and 10(2) and (3).

These repeals have effect in accordance with section 36 of, and Schedule 6 to, this Act.

(12) DISTRIBUTIONS: CONSEQUENTIAL REPEALS

Chapter	Short title	Extent of repeal
1997 c 16	The Finance Act 1997	In Schedule 7, paragraphs 1 and 7.

1   The repeal of paragraph 1 of Schedule 7 to the Finance Act 1997 has effect in relation to distributions made on or after 6th April 1999.

2   The repeal of paragraph 7 of that Schedule has effect in relation to payments which are representative of distributions made on or after 6th April 1999.

(13) INTEREST ON GILT-EDGED SECURITIES, ETC

Chapter	Short title	Extent of repeal
1988 c 1	The Income and Corporation Taxes Act 1988	In section 50(1), paragraphs (*a*), (*c*) and (*d*). Section 51A. In section 118G— (*a*) in subsection (3), paragraphs (*b*) and (*d*) to (f); (*b*) subsections (8) and (10); and (*c*) in subsection (9), the words "or (8)", "or subject to deduction of tax at a reduced rate" and "subsection (10) below and to". In section 118H— (*a*) in subsection (2), the words from "or (8), or" to the words "case may be" in the first place where they occur and the words "or (8)" in the second place where they occur; and (*b*) in subsections (3) and (4), the words "or (8)", wherever they occur.

Chapter	Short title	Extent of repeal
1995 c 4	The Finance Act 1995	Section 77.

These repeals have effect in relation to payments falling due on or after 6th April 1998.

(14) GROUP RELIEF

Chapter	Short title	Extent of repeal
1988 c 1	The Income and Corporation Taxes Act 1988	Section 403(9) Sections 408 and 409. Section 411(2) to (9).
1990 c 29	The Finance Act 1990	Section 96(11).

These repeals have effect, subject to the provisions of paragraph 9 of Schedule 7 to this Act, for accounting periods ending on or after 2nd July 1997.

PART III
STATUTORY EFFECT OF RESOLUTIONS ETC

Chapter	Short title	Extent of repeal
1993 c 34	The Finance Act 1993	Section 206(3).

INDEX

All references are to F(No 2)A 1997 unless otherwise stated

167

Index

L

LLOYD'S UNDERWRITERS
premiums trust funds, restriction on entitlement to tax credits, s 22
special reserve funds, tax credits and, s 34, Sch 4 para 30

LOAN RELATIONSHIPS
carry-back,
    generally, s 40
    insurance companies, in case of, s 40(3)–(6)
    non-trade deficits, s 40(2)

LOSSES
relief for,
    group relief, restrictions on, s 41, Sch 7
    loan relationship deficits, carry-back, s 40
    trading losses, carry-back, s 39
windfall tax, deduction for purposes of computing losses, s 3(3)

M

MEDICAL INSURANCE PREMIUMS
withdrawal of relief on, s 17

MORTGAGE INTEREST PAYMENTS
relief,
    deduction at source, s 15(2), (3)
    loans to buy land etc, s 15(1), (3)

O

OVERSEA LIFE INSURANCE COMPANY
tax credits, s 34, Sch 4 para 29

P

PAYING AGENT
withholding provisions, amendments to, s 38

PENSION FUNDS
tax credits, restrictions on use of, s 19

PERSONAL REPRESENTATIVE
company distributions, income consisting of, tax treatment, s 33

PLANT AND MACHINERY
hire-purchase by finance lessor, capital allowance consequences, s 45
sale and leaseback, restriction on capital allowances, s 46

PROFIT-RELATED PAY SCHEME
"existing scheme": meaning, s 4(6)
windfall tax, effect, s 4

PROFITS
windfall tax, deduction for purposes of computing profits, s 3(3)

R

RESIDUARY ESTATE
taxation of income from, s 33

S

SCHEDULE F
income chargeable under,
    highest part of person's income, treatment as, 31(4)
    ordinary rate, s 31(1), (2)
    rates of tax applicable to, s 31(5)

Index

TRADING LOSSES
carry-back,
  apportionment rules, s 39(5)
  company reconstructions without a change of ownership, s 39(7)
  generally, s 39
  reduction of carry-back period, s 39(2)
  three-year carry-back period in certain cases, s 39(3)

TRANSFER OF ASSETS ABROAD
liability to tax, s 34, Sch 4 para 20

U

UNIT TRUSTS
unauthorised, distributions received by, treatment as foreign income dividend, s 29

W

WINDFALL TAX
administration and collection, s 3, Sch 2
appeals,
  assessments and decisions on claims, against, s 3, Sch 2 para 9
  powers of Special Commissioners on, s 3, Sch 2 para 10
  procedures on, s 3, Sch 2 para 11
assessments,
  double assessments, claim to relieve, s 3, Sch 2 para 7
  general power to make, s 3, Sch 2 para 4
  generally, s 3, Sch 2 para 6
  unassessed liabilities, power to make assessments on discovery of, s 3, Sch 2 para 5
charge to, s 1
companies liable to, s 2
deduction in computing income etc, s 3(3)
errors or mistakes in returns etc, claims to correct, s 3, Sch 2 para 8
false information, penalties for furnishing, s 3, Sch 2 para 14
generally, s 1, Sch 2 paras 18, 19
information, collection of, s 3, Sch 2 para 13
interest provisions, s 3, Sch 2 para 12
payment of tax, s 3, Sch 2 para 3
penalties,
  false information, for furnishing, s 3, Sch 2 para 14
  general provisions, s 1, Sch 2 para 17
profit-related pay schemes, and, s 4
quantification of privatisation windfall,
  apportionment for purposes of determining initial period, s 1, Sch 1 para 6(4)–(6)
  basic rule, s 1, Sch 1 para 1
  company privatised in stages, s 1, Sch 1 para 4
  demerged successors and predecessors, apportionment between, s 1, Sch 1 para 7
  disposal for privatisation purposes, value put on, s 1, Sch 1 para 3
  generally, s 1, Sch 1 para 8
  "initial period": meaning, s 1, Sch 1 para 6(1)–(3)
  total profits for initial period, s 1, Sch 1 para 5
  value of disposal in profit-making terms, s 1, Sch 1 para 2
quantifying windfall, s 1(3)
rate, s 1(2)
recovery of tax,
  generally, s 3, Sch 2 para 15
  group members, against, s 3, Sch 2 para 16
returns
  generally, s 3, Sch 2 para 1
  liability and failure to make, notification, s 3, Sch 2 para 2